Praise for *The Partly Cloudy Patriot*

"Snappy humor goes well with provocative thinking about the politics of connection."

—*The Kansas City Star*

"Charming, funny, and blessed with a knack for finding absurdities in mundane scenarios."

—*The Sunday Oregonian*

"An irresistible mix of acerbic wit and semi-apologetic fanaticism."

—*Austin American-Statesman*

"Her gift is one of cosmic inclusion—allowing the natural collision of intellect and personality, rigorous research and generational quirks, dual obsessions with presidential libraries and Pop-a-Shot basketball."

—*The Boston Globe*

"Sassy, learned pieces . . . [Vowell is] distinctive, excitable, and odd in a good way. Refreshingly, Vowell doesn't just have opinions; she has beliefs. . . . A singular mixture of whimsy, honesty, and seriousness."

—*The Atlanta Journal-Constitution*

"Vowell reveals herself to be a master at ferreting out the contradictions and hypocrisies that are unique to American democracy."

—*Time Out New York*

"An engrossing take on the suddenly sexy topic of love of country . . . a work of humor, nuance, and restrained passion, managing both to discuss America's flaws and restore readers' pride in the nation. Vowell puts the reader on notice that, sure, she's funny, but supporting the quips is a rock-solid knowledge of history. Refreshing, inspiring, enchanting."

—*Kirkus* (starred review)

"No one in recent memory has been as insightful on the direct pleasures and perils of voting, the misuse of Rosa Parks as a metaphor, the appeal of Canadians, and the relative merits of presidential libraries . . . eloquent . . . hilarious. . . . Vowell, like David Sedaris, goes too far, cares too much, and remains a very anxious and extremely funny citizen and shady patriot."

—*Publishers Weekly*

THE PARTLY CLOUDY PATRIOT

SARAH VOWELL

SIMON & SCHUSTER

new york london toronto sydney

SIMON & SCHUSTER
Rockefeller Center
1230 Avenue of the Americas
New York, NY 10020

First Simon & Schuster trade paperback edition 2003

SIMON & SCHUSTER and colophon are registered trademarks of Simon & Schuster, Inc.

Designed by Jeanette Olender

For information regarding special discounts for bulk purchases, please contact
Simon & Schuster Special Sales at 1-800-456-6798 or business@simonandschuster.com

Manufactured in the United States of America

10 9 8 7 6 5 4

The Library of Congress has cataloged the hardcover edition as follows:
    Vowell, Sarah.
        The partly cloudy patriot / Sarah Vowell.
            p. cm.
            1. United States—History—Anecdotes. 2. United States—Politics and
government—Anecdotes. 3. United States—Description and travel—Anecdotes.
4. National characteristics, American—Anecdotes. 5. Vowell, Sarah, 1969– —
Anecdotes. I. Title
E178.6.V68 2002
973—dc21   2002066988
ISBN 0-7432-2352-7
        0-7432-4380-3 (Pbk)

These pieces first appeared in the following places: "The First Thanksgiving," "Ike Was
a Handsome Man," "Democracy and Things Like That," and "Underground Lunchroom" (with support from *Hearing Voices*) on *This American Life;* "The New German
Cinema" in *Esquire;* "Pop-A-Shot" in *Forbes ASAP;* "Dear Dead Congressman" in *Open
Letters;* "Rosa Parks, *C'est Moi*" in *Time;* "Tom Cruise Makes Me Nervous" and "Wonder Twins" in *Salon;* and "Tom Landry, Existentialist, Dead at 75" in *McSweeney's.*

TO **A**MY

After every great battle, a great storm. Even civic events, the same. On Saturday last, a forenoon like whirling demons, dark, with slanting rain, full of rage; and then the afternoon, so calm, so bathed with flooding splendor from heaven's most excellent sun, with atmosphere of sweetness; so clear, it show'd the stars, long, long before they were due. As the President came out on the Capitol portico, a curious little white cloud, the only one in that part of the sky, appear'd like a hovering bird, right over him.

—Walt Whitman, witnessing Lincoln's Second Inaugural Address, *Memoranda During the War*

CONTENTS

THE PARTLY CLOUDY PATRIOT

What He Said There

There are children playing soccer on a field at Gettysburg where the Union Army lost the first day's fight. Playing soccer, like a bunch of Belgians—and in the middle of football season no less. Outside of town, there's a billboard for a shopping mall said to be "*The* Gettysburg Address For Shopping." Standing on the train platform where Abraham Lincoln disembarked from Washington on November 18, 1863, there's a Confederate soldier, a reenactor. "Which direction is south?" I ask him, trying to re-create the presidential moment. When the fake Johnny Reb replies that he doesn't know, I scold him, "Dude, you're from there!" Around the corner, the citizens of Gettysburg stand in line at the Majestic Theater for the 2:10 showing of *Meet the Parents*. Bennett, the friend I'm with, makes a dumb joke about Lincoln meeting his in-laws, the Todds. "Things did not go well," he says.

It is November 19, 2000, the 137th anniversary of the cemetery dedication ceremony at which Lincoln delivered a certain speech. "Four score and seven years ago," Lincoln said, referring to the Declaration of Independence in 1776, "our fathers brought forth on this continent a new nation, conceived in Liberty, and dedicated to the proposition that all men are created equal." Always start with the good news.

I could say that I've come to Gettysburg as a rubbernecking tourist, that I've shown up to force myself to mull over the consequences of a war I never think about. Because that would make a better story—a gum-chewing, youngish person who says "like" too much, comes face to face with the horrors of war and Learns Something. But, like, this story isn't like that. Fact is, I think about the Civil War all the time, every day. I can't even use a cotton ball to remove my eye makeup without spacing out about slavery's favorite cash crop and that line from Lincoln's Second Inaugural Address that "it may seem strange that any men should dare to ask a just God's assistance in wringing their bread from the sweat of other men's faces." Well, that, and why does black eyeliner smudge way more than brown?

I guess Gettysburg is a pilgrimage. And, like all pilgrims, I'm a mess. You don't cross state lines to attend the 137th anniversary of anything unless something's missing in your life.

The fighting at Gettysburg took place between July 1 and July 3, 1863. The Union, under the command of General George Meade, won. But not at first, and not with ease. In the biggest, bloodiest battle ever fought on U.S. soil, 51,000 men were killed, wounded, or missing. I am interested enough in that whopping statistic to spend most of the day being driven

around the immense battlefield. Interested enough to walk down a spur on Little Round Top to see the monument to the 20th Maine, where a bookish but brave college professor named Joshua Lawrence Chamberlain ran out of ammo and ordered the bayonets that held the Union's ground. Interested enough to stop at the Copse of Trees—where the Confederate General George Pickett aimed his thousands of soldiers who were mowed down at the climax—and sit on a rock and wonder how many Southern skulls were cracked open on it.

I care enough about the 51,000 to visit the graves, semicircular rows of stones with the otherwise forgotten names of Jeremiah Davis and Jesse Wills and Wesley Raikes laid right next to Hiram Hughes. And the little marble cubes engraved with numbers assigned the unknown. Who was 811? Or 775? The markers for the unknowns are so minimal and so beautiful I catch myself thinking of these men as sculptures. Here, they are called "bodies." There are slabs chiseled MASSACHU-SETTS 159 BODIES and CONNECTICUT 22 BODIES and WISCONSIN 73 BODIES.

So I pay my respects to the bodies, but I'll admit that I am more concerned with the 272 words President Lincoln said about them. The best the slaughtered can usually hope for is a cameo in some kind of art. Mostly, we living need a *Guernica* to remind us of Guernica. In the Gettysburg Address, Lincoln said of the men who shed their blood, "The world will little note, nor long remember, what we say here, but it can never forget what they did here." Who did he think he was kidding? We only think of them because of him. Robert E. Lee high-tailed it out of Gettysburg on the Fourth of July, the same day the Confederates surrendered Vicksburg to U. S. Grant—a big deal at the time because it gave the Feds control of the Mississippi. And yet who these days dwells on Vicksburg, except for the park rangers who work there and a handful of sore losers who whine when they're asked to take the stars and bars off their godforsaken state flags?

The Gettysburg Address is more than a eulogy. It's a soybean, a versatile little problem solver that can be processed into seemingly infinite, ingenious products. In this speech, besides cleaning up the founding fathers' slavery mess by calling for a "new birth of freedom," Lincoln comforted grieving mothers who would never bounce grandchildren on their knees and ran for reelection at the same time. Lest we forget, he came to Washington from Illinois. Even though we think of him as the American Jesus, he had a little Mayor Daley in him too. Lincoln the politician needed the win at Gettysburg and, on the cusp of an election year, he wanted to remind the people *explicitly* that they could win the war if they just held on, while *implicitly* reminding them to use their next presidential ballot to write their commander in chief a thank-you note.

Privately, Lincoln has mixed feelings about Gettysburg because he's certain the war could have ended right here if only General Meade had not let General Lee get away. According to a letter written right after the battle, Lincoln is "deeply mortified" that "Meade and his noble army had expended all the skill, and toil, and blood, up to the ripe harvest, and then let the crop go to waste." Because Lincoln is a good man, he does not say this in front of the families who came to the cemetery to hear that their loved ones "shall not have died in vain." Because he is a good politician, he looks on the bright side. Though I personally suspect that in Lincoln's first draft, the line about how "it is for us the living, rather, to be dedicated here to the unfinished work which they who fought here have thus far so nobly advanced" was simply "Goddamn fucking Meade."

Abraham Lincoln is one of my favorite writers. "The mystic chords of memory." "Better angels of our nature." "The father of waters flows unvexed to the sea." All those brilliant phrases I'd admired for so long, and yet I never truly thought of him as a writer until I visited the David Wills house in Gettysburg's town square.

In 1863, Wills was charged by Pennsylvania's governor to oversee the battlefield's cleanup and the construction of the cemetery. His house, now a museum, is where Lincoln stayed the night before delivering the address. I walk into the room where Lincoln slept, with its flowerdy carpet and flowerdy walls, with its canopy bed and its water pitcher and towels, and for several minutes the only possible thought is that he was here. There's the window he leaned out of the night of the 18th, teasing the crowd outside that he had nothing to say. And, this being a sweet old-fashioned tourist trap, there's a gangly Lincoln mannequin in white shirtsleeves, hunched over a small table, his long legs poking out the side. He's polishing the speech. The myth is that he wrote it on the back of an envelope on the train, but probably he's been slaving over it for days and days. Still, he doesn't finish it until he's in this room, the morning of the 19th, the morning he's to deliver it.

To say that Abraham Lincoln was a writer is to say that he

was a procrastinator. How many deadlines have I nearly blown over the years, slumped like Lincoln, fretting over words that didn't come out until almost too late? Of course, the stakes are lower when one is under pressure to think up insightful things to say about the new Brad Pitt movie instead of, say, saving the Union. On the other hand, I've whipped out Aerosmith record reviews that are longer than the Gettysburg Address, so where's *my* mannequin?

Looking at Lincoln rushing to stave off failure, I felt so close to him. Or let's say I felt closer. My grandest hope for my own hastily written sentences is that they would keep a stranger company on an airplane. Abraham Lincoln could turn a pretty phrase such as "I invoke the considerate judgment of mankind" and put it in the proclamation that *freed the slaves*. Even Mailer wouldn't claim to top that.

At the Gettysburg National Cemetery, there's a ceremony every November 19 to celebrate the anniversary of Lincoln's speech. I sit down on a folding chair among the shivering townspeople. A brass band from Gettysburg High School plays the national anthem. The eminent Yale historian James McPherson delivers a speech he may have written a long time ago to make college students feel bad. Because when he accuses the audience of taking our democracy for granted, there's a rustling in the crowd. While people who commemorate the anniversary of the Gettysburg Address surely have a lot of problems, taking democracy for granted isn't one of them. New Jersey's governor, Christine Todd Whitman, then takes the podium, proclaiming, "Our government doesn't have all the answers, and it never will." That is code for "Sorry about that icky photo that shows me laughing as I frisk an innocent black man on a State Police ride-along."

I sit through all of this, impatient. I didn't come here for the opening acts. Like a Van Halen concertgoer who doesn't high-five his friend until he hears the first bar of "Jump," all I've been waiting for is for the Lincoln impersonator James Getty to stand up and read the Gettysburg Address already. This is what Garry Wills says happened after Lincoln stopped talking in 1863: "The crowd departed with a new thing in its ideological luggage, that new constitution Lincoln had substituted for the one they brought there with them. They walked off, from those curving graves on the hillside, under a changed sky, into a different America." This is what happened after the Lincoln impersonator stopped talking in the year 2000: The eight-year-old boy sitting next to me pointed at Getty and asked his mom, "Isn't that guy too short?"

I glance at the kid with envy. He's at that first, great, artsy-craftsy age when Americans learn about Abraham Lincoln. How many of us drew his beard in crayon? We built models of his boyhood cabin with Elmer's glue and toothpicks. We memorized the Gettysburg Address, reciting its ten sentences in stovepipe hats stapled out of black construction paper. The teachers taught us to like Washington and to respect Jefferson. But Lincoln—him they taught us to love.

The First Thanksgiving

When I invited my mom and dad to come to New York City to have Thanksgiving at my house, I never expected them to say yes. Not only had they never been to New York, they had never been east of the Mississippi. Nor had they ever visited me. I've always had these fantasies about being in a normal family in which the parents come to town and their adult daughter spends their entire visit daydreaming of suicide. I'm here to tell you that dreams really do come true.

I was terrified we wouldn't have enough to talk about. In the interest of harmony, there's a tacit agreement in my family; the following subjects are best avoided in any conversation longer than a minute and a half: national politics, state and local politics, any music by any person who never headlined at the Grand Ole Opry, my personal life, and their so-called god. Five whole days. When I visit them back home in Montana, conversation isn't a problem because we go to the movies every afternoon. That way, we can be together but without the burden of actually talking to each other. Tommy Lee Jones, bless his heart, does the talking for us.

But my sister, Amy, is coming and bringing her lively seven-month-old son, Owen, along, so the cinema's not an option. Which means five days together—just us—no movies. We are heading into uncharted and possibly hostile waters, pioneers in a New World. It is Thanksgiving. The pilgrims had the *Mayflower*. I buy a gravy boat.

It's lucky that Amy's coming with Mom and Dad. Amy still lives six blocks away from them in Bozeman. She would act as interpreter and go-between among my parents and me. Like Squanto.

Amy's husband, Jay, has decided to stay home in Montana to go deer hunting with his brother. Everyone else arrives at my apartment in Chelsea. Amy and Owen are bunking with me, so I walk my parents around the corner to check them into their hotel on Twenty-third.

"Here we are," says Mom, stopping under the awning of the Chelsea Hotel. There she stands, a woman whose favorite book is called, simply, Matthew, right on the spot where the cops hauled Sid Vicious out in handcuffs after his girlfriend was found stabbed to death on their hotel room floor.

"No, Mother," I say, taking her arm and directing her down the block to the Chelsea Savoy, a hotel where they go to the trouble to clean the rooms each day.

It is around this time, oh, twenty minutes into their trip, that my dad starts making wisecracks like "Boy, kid, bet you can't wait until we're out of here." My father, a man who

moved us sixteen hundred miles away from our Oklahoma rel-
atives so he wouldn't have to see them anymore, makes a joke
on average every two hours he is here about how much I'm an-
ticipating the second they'll say good-bye. I find this charming
but so disturbingly true I don't know what to say.

By halfway through the first day, I discover I needn't have
worried what we would talk about, with the baby preventing us
from seeing movies. When you have a baby around, the baby is
the movie. We occupy an entire entertaining hour just on
drool, nonnarrative drool. At this stage, baby Owen is laughing, sitting up, and able to roll over. He is the cutest, the funniest, sweetest, smartest, best-behaved baby in the world.

Then there's the sightseeing. First stop, Ellis Island. The
thing about going to Ellis Island is that it's a lot like going to
Ellis Island. Perhaps to help you better understand the immi-
grant experience, they make you stand in line for the crammed
ferry for an hour and a half in the windy cold. By the time
we step onto the island, we are huddled masses yearning to
breathe free.

Our great-grandmother Ellen passed through here on her
way from Sweden. We watch a video on the health inspections
given to immigrants, walk past oodles of photos of men in hats
and women in shawls. Though no one says anything, I know
my father and mother and sister are thinking what I'm thinking. They're thinking about when we moved away from Oklahoma to Montana, how unknown that was, how strange and
lonesome. I read a letter in a display case that says, "And I
never saw my mother again," and I think of my grandfather,
how we just drove off, leaving him behind, waving to us in the

11

rearview mirror. And here we are in New York, because here I am in New York, because ever since Ellen's father brought her here, every generation moves away from the one before.

It is curious that we Americans have a holiday—Thanksgiving—that's all about people who left their homes for a life of their own choosing, a life that was different from their parents' lives. And how do we celebrate it? By hanging out with our parents! It's as if on the Fourth of July we honored our independence from the British by barbecuing crumpets.

Just as Amy and I grew up and left our parents, someday Owen will necessarily grow up and ditch my sister. And, appropriately enough, it is on this weekend that Owen spends the very first night of his life away from his mother. My parents baby-sit while Amy and I go to a rock show. Owen lives through it, as does she, though she talks about him all night, which I guess is how it goes.

Thanksgiving morning, my parents take Owen to see the Macy's parade while Amy and I start making dinner. Let me repeat that—my mother leaves while I cook. Specifically, cornbread dressing, a dish my mother has made every Thanksgiving since before I was born. To her credit, she has not inquired about my process since she phoned to ask me if she should bring cornmeal in her suitcase. As an Okie, my mom only uses white cornmeal processed by the Shawnee Company in Muskogee. She does not even consider my cornbread to be cornbread at all because I make it with yellow cornmeal and, heresy, sugar. "You don't make cornbread," she told me, in the same deflated voice she uses to describe my hair. "You make johnny cake."

I'm standing at the cutting board chopping sage and it hits me what it means that she is letting me be in charge of the dressing: I am going to die. Being in charge of the dressing means you are a grown-up for real, and being a grown-up for real means you're getting old and getting old means you are definitely, finally, totally going to die. My mother is a grand-mother and my sister is a mother and I have decided the dressing will be yellow this year, therefore, we'll all be dead someday.

"Is that enough celery?" Amy asks, pointing to a green mound on the counter. Is there ever enough celery? Do my parents have more celery in their past than they do in their fu-ture? Do I?

I have invited my friends John and David to join us for din-ner, and I was a little nervous about how everyone would get along. To my delight, the meal is smooth and congenial. My friends and I talk about the West Nile virus killing birds on Long Island. My father counters with a lovely anecdote about an open copper pit in Butte that filled up with contaminated rainwater and killed 250 geese in one day. There is nothing like eating one dead bird and talking about a bunch of other dead birds to really bring people together.

The next morning, right about the time Owen starts to cry while—simultaneously—my mother jams the bathroom door and my father's on his hands and knees prying it open with a penknife, a cloud passes over me. Once or twice a day, I am enveloped inside what I like to call the Impenetrable Shield of Melancholy. This shield, it is impenetrable. Hence the name. I cannot speak. And while I can feel myself freeze up, I can't do

13

anything about it. As my family fusses, I spend an inordinate amount of time pretending to dry my hair, the bedroom door closed, the hair dryer on full blast, pointed at nothing.

Everybody in the family goes through these little spells. I just happen to be the spooky one at this particular moment. When people ask me if I'm the black sheep of the family I always say that, no, we're all black sheep. Every few hours they're here, I look over at my dad, nervously crunching his fingers together. If he were at home for Thanksgiving, he'd be ignoring us and spending all his time in his shop. I watch him move his fingers in the air and realize he's turning some hunk of metal on an imaginary lathe.

The thing that unites us is that all four of us are homebody claustrophobes who prefer to be alone and are suspicious of other people. So the trait that binds us together as a family— preferring to keep to ourselves—makes it difficult to *be* together as a family. Paradoxically, it's at these times that I feel closest to them, that I understand them best, that I love them most. It's just surprising we ever breed.

The next day, we do the most typical thing we could possibly do as a family. We split up. I stay home cleaning, Mom goes to Macy's, Amy and Owen visit the Museum of Modern Art, and Dad tours Teddy Roosevelt's birthplace. By the time we all reconvene on Saturday evening, my ragged mother becomes so ambitious with her sightseeing that I can tell she's decided that she's never coming back. "Do you guys want to see Rockefeller Center?" I ask, and she says, "Yeah, because who knows when I'll be back again." Ditto the Empire State Building, "because who knows when I'll be back again."

If you are visiting the Empire State Building, may I offer some advice? If you are waiting in the very long line for the very last elevator and an attendant says that anyone who wants to walk up the last six flights may do so now, right away, and you are with your aging parents and a sister who is carrying a child the size of a fax machine, stay in the line for the elevator. But if you must take the stairs, go first, and do not look back; otherwise your parents will look like one of those Renaissance frescoes of Adam and Eve being expelled from the Garden of Eden, all hunched over and afraid.

So we make it to the observation deck, Brooklyn to the south of us, New Jersey to the west, places that people fled to from far away, places that people now run away from, to make another life. It's dark and cold and windy, and we're sweaty from climbing the stairs. It's really pretty though. And there we stand, side by side, sharing a thought like the family we are. My sister wishes she were home. My mom and dad wish they were home. I wish they were home too.

Ike Was a Handsome Man

emo
To: Former President William Jefferson Clinton
From: Citizen Sarah Jane Vowell
Re: Presidential libraries fact-finding tour

Mr. President, I'm tired. Who wouldn't be after a decade of sticking up for you? I am looking forward to your presidential library in Little Rock because I am worn-out from defending you. I would like to donate what's left of my faith to some building in Arkansas, where it can be archived in an acid-free box, so I can make a little extra room in my heart and fill it up with trying not to hate your successor. But before relinquishing my duties as your crabby little cheerleader, I scoped out four presidential libraries to help you figure out how to do the job right. Not that you asked me. I just don't want you to mess this up.

We'll begin our tour at the John F. Kennedy Library overlooking Boston Harbor. Partly because your youth and flash have been described as "Kennedyesque," and partly because you yourself have often invoked the comparison, most notably by trotting out that film of you as a teenager shaking JFK's hand, an image of eerie destiny.

I talked to the Kennedy library's curator, Frank Rigg. We agreed that the plainest pleasure of visiting presidential libraries is getting close to the actual stuff of history. For example, the presidential cheat sheet for the pronunciation of a certain German phrase. Rigg tells me, "We have on display in one of the cases in that room the little card on which he's written 'Ich bin ein Berliner' spelled out phonetically. If you watch the film [of his Berlin speech], you can see that just before he gets to the line he looks down at the paper and then looks up and says, 'Ich bin ein Berliner.' I love those little correspondences between an artifact and a piece of film. The most beautiful one comes towards the end of the museum, where we have the video of his tour of Ireland in 1963. As he was leaving, he quoted a piece of poetry that Mrs. De Valera, the wife of the president of Ireland, had recited to him the night before at dinner. He'd written it down on the back of his itinerary."

On the video, Kennedy says that Mrs. De Valera "quoted this poem and I wrote down the words because I thought they were beautiful." Rigg points out how "you see him in the film pick up a piece of paper that he has under a silver jug. It's windy. That's why he has it under there. He picks it up and then he recites the beautiful lines." Kennedy quoted, " 'Thus return from travels long. Years of exile. Years of pain. To see old Shannon's face again.' Well, I'm going to try to come back and see old Shannon's face again." Rigg continues, "At the end, he folds it up and you can see the crease. And again it's one of those things where you feel as if you're there in that moment in time."

In this I. M. Pei–designed white box, JFK's life and death unfold primarily on television monitors and video screens. I walk in suspicious. I have never particularly worshiped Jack Kennedy. I mean, he didn't really do anything. Except talk. He spoke of civil rights, but it was Lyndon Johnson who got actual laws passed. And then there's the minor matter of the Cuban Missile Crisis, perhaps the scariest single week in the history of the world. And yet, at JFK's library, I found myself hoodwinked by pretty words. I stood there, transfixed by the film of his Inaugural Address:

> Now the trumpet summons us again—not as a call to bear arms, though arms we need—not as a call to battle, though embattled we are—but a call to bear the burden of a long twilight struggle, year in and year out, "rejoicing in hope, patient in tribulation"—a struggle against the common enemies of man: tyranny, poverty, disease, and war itself. . . . With a good conscience our only sure reward, with history the final judge of our deeds, let us go forth to lead the land we love, asking His blessing and His help, but knowing that here on earth God's work must truly be our own.

"As you may have noticed," Rigg says, "there are no narrators to our films and our videos. The principal voice is that of John F. Kennedy himself. And we did that very consciously."

19

There are also a lot of pretty pictures—home movies of JFK handing a dandelion to John-John, one weirdly evocative film-strip of the president in which all he does is carry a briefcase and walk to a car. I watch it wondering, Why is this so riveting? He's taking work home. But I can't resist him. The man is Medusa: Don't look in his eyes.

President Clinton, you should milk this in your library. Where the legislative record is perhaps ambiguous, or down-right shabby, go for the flashy sound bites. You are such a sweet talker, the Charlie Parker of the press conference Q & A, riffing rhythmically about everything from interest rates to Greece versus Turkey with regards to Cyprus. There are prob-ably too many momentous quotes to sift through, but placing all the State of the Union Addresses on video loops is a good place to start. My personal favorite was the one in 1997 in which you proclaimed, "America is far more than a place. It is an idea—the most powerful idea in the history of nations. And all of us in this Chamber, we are now the bearers of that idea, leading a great people into a New World." There was one para-graph in your speech at the Oklahoma City bombing memorial service that actually made me want to be a better person. You said, "When there is talk of hatred, let us stand up and talk against it. When there is talk of violence, let us stand up and talk against it. In the face of death let us honor life." And I al-ways thought one of your loveliest moments as president was one of your smallest. Might your librarians dig up a tape of that special you did for the music channel VH1 in your second term called *Bill Clinton: Rock 'n' Roll President*? There was one scene in which you were flipping through your old records, reminiscing about what music has meant to you. Your face lit up when you spotted a Ray Charles album in the stack. It was a fleeting, seemingly trivial clip, and yet the way you beamed at the cover and said Ray Charles's name revealed your ability to revere.

I wanted to go to the Dwight David Eisenhower Library in Abilene, Kansas, to see how they handle something the Clinton Presidential Center will have to tackle. Which is, if one of the achievements of a presidency is economic prosperity, how can that be displayed without trotting out a bunch of toasters and hula hoops? Without making people seem dumb and materialistic? How do you convey the decency of making people's lives better? Unfortunately for our project, the way the Eisenhower library deals with this challenge is—they basically ignore it. In fact, you'd barely know the man was president. The exhibit devoted to his White House years mostly consists of heaps of weird but swanky gifts he got, like a mosaic desk from the shah of Iran. The museum is great at Eisenhower's military career. I walk around with its director, Dan Holt, who points out "the original note that Roosevelt and Churchill signed appointing Eisenhower the Supreme Commander." We pass a documentary in which a corny narrator calls Ike "a military meteor on the rise" and I think, Who cares if he accomplished anything after V-J Day?

There is a lesson to be learned here after all. Mr. President, play to your strengths. Eisenhower's greatest achievement was liberating Europe. Your greatest achievement? Balancing the budget. Not as dramatic, I know. They're probably not going to make a Tom Hanks movie about fiscal policy, no matter how inspired that fiscal policy might be. But still, as your White House Web page cheerfully pointed out, your money wrangling did result in the longest economic expansion in U.S. history, the lowest unemployment rate in thirty years, and the most new jobs ever created in a single administration.

In the Eisenhower library, the climax of the visit is D day, in which you turn a sharp corner and, suddenly, you're standing like a soldier on a ship's ramp, facing a Normandy beach. My tour guide, Dan Holt, walks me across "a small mock-up of an LCI (landing craft infantry) and into the photograph that's been called the Jaws of Death, which is the landings at Omaha Beach."

As we trudge across the ramp, we glimpse our buddies ahead of us, slogging through the bloody wet, and the beach so far away. In short, this is very effective theater. Which leads me to my next recommendation, Mr. Clinton. What about a similar stage set, only in your library, instead of being a soldier leaving the boat for Omaha Beach, the visitor could walk in the shoes of Fed Chairman Alan Greenspan, as he steps out of a Lincoln Town Car and into the Dirksen Senate Office Building to endorse the Clinton deficit reduction strategy before the Senate Banking Committee!

A word on the people who run these libraries, Mr. President. Fortunately for you, they are very attached to their subjects, very loyal. Their president becomes a kind of mental roommate. And each of the library directors I interviewed spoke of his president with affection, like a mom almost.

Dan Holt praises Ike's correspondence skill: "He was a wonderful letter writer."

And talks up his private-sector prowess: "He was an outstanding businessman."

His book learning: "His grammar was very good."

His looks: "He was a very handsome man."

All the loyalty you would want while you're in office you finally get after you quit. None of the library directors have written kiss-and-tell memoirs and gone on to work for ABC.

I ask Holt if he has any advice for the administrators of the new presidential library in Little Rock. "Bigger rest rooms," he says, "and more drinking fountains. But I think you have to have fun. I'm a true believer in that. There have to be bells and whistles."

In the bells and whistles department, the Lyndon Baines Johnson Library and Museum in Austin, Texas, features a little piece of Disney World in the form of an LBJ animatron. It is a Lyndon Johnson robot, a robot who wears cowboy garb and tells folksy stories. Have you heard the one about the man who goes to a doctor because he's hard of hearing? The doctor advises the man to quit drinking and sends him home. A few days later, the man returns to the doctor's office. He hasn't stopped his drinking. According to the LBJ robot, the doctor scolds the man, asking, "'Didn't I tell you when you were here that you should cut out your drinking if you wanted to improve your hearing?' He said, 'Yes.' 'Well, why didn't you do it?' He said, 'Doctor, when I got home and I considered it, I just decided that I liked what I drank so much better than what I heard.'"

The library's director, Harry Middleton, who is showing me around, turns a corner and says, "As we move into this area, we show some of the correspondence that President Johnson got, some of it quite critical, some of it quite supportive."

One letter hanging on the wall is addressed to Lyndon Johnson from one Frances Mercer of Beverly Hills, California. She wrote, "Mr. President—you have engaged this country in an act of war, without the consent of Congress. I consider having worked for your campaign one of the most tragic mistakes of my life."

President Clinton, I am going to hazard a guess that you yourself have received one or two angry letters. The question arises: What are you going to do about all the people who hate your guts, not to put too fine a point on it. What are you going to do about all the aspects of your presidency you'd rather forget about?

I tell Harry Middleton that I heard a rumor that in the initial exhibition at the LBJ library, there was little or no representation of Vietnam and that the president himself came to the library and insisted that that part of the exhibition should be beefed up.

Middleton nods. "To a certain extent that's true. There was a representation of Vietnam. But nothing that showed the controversy of Vietnam. And when President Johnson walked through the library just a few weeks before it was to open, one of the things that he commented on was that the library did not indicate how contentious that time was. He said to me, 'That was a very controversial period. We've got to make sure that people know that we understand that.' He said to me, 'I don't want another damn credibility gap.' "

"Do you think the people who are in charge of a president's

legacy are more apt to protect him than the president himself would be of his own legacy?"

"Yeah," he says. "Unless you get a clear direction from the president that he wants it all laid out. In the case of Johnson, I've been director here from the beginning. On one occasion when he was concerned that we might be too protective he said to me, 'Good men have been trying to protect my reputation for forty years, and not a damn one has succeeded. What makes you think you can?' So we have not tried to do that."

Mr. Clinton, here's a list of things you should not white-wash. Before we even discuss the scandals, let's talk about the ordinary failures: What about one of your key campaign promises, to reform health care? A fiasco. Ditto Waco. Or the 1994 congressional elections, in which the voting public punched Republican names on their ballots with one hand, while using the other hand to give you the finger. I'm not even mentioning all the half-ass policies like Don't Ask Don't Tell, or Bosnia or Somalia.

Finally, you *did* have sexual relations with that woman. You have to confront this. I do not know how. What I do know is that if your library's only exhibits from 1998 are celebrations of the budget surplus and a copy of the Wye River Memorandum between Netanyahu and Arafat, those of us who lived through that excruciating impeachment trial are going to feel cheated. I suppose everyone has a favorite artifact from that era (insert stained dress joke here), but I always thought that gift of Walt Whitman's *Leaves of Grass* that you gave to your mistress helped me understand you better. Perhaps your exhibition designers can do something with a line or two from "Song of My-

25

self." No, not "Smile, for your lover comes." The best description of you I've ever read was published in 1855:

> Do I contradict myself?
> Very well then I contradict myself,
> (I am large, I contain multitudes.)

Mr. President, take heart. Someday, there might be people in this country who think that cheating on your wife and lying about it is not as embarrassing as being one of the presidents who got 58,000 American soldiers killed, not to mention more than 3 million Vietnamese.

Harry Middleton insists, "I think that a library should not proselytize. It should not sugarcoat and should not distort the facts or the truth in order to hide a controversy surrounding the president. Otherwise, it's just not fair to the public."

Meanwhile, in Yorba Linda, California: "First of all, I don't think a presidential library should necessarily bend over backwards to be objective and fair and inclusive of every important telling fact on all sides of the argument."

This is John Taylor, director of the Richard Nixon Library and Birthplace. It's about a fifteen-minute drive from Disneyland. Just as Harry Middleton of the LBJ library is doing his job according to LBJ's wishes, John Taylor is doing his job the way Nixon would want. He tells me, "People expect presidential libraries to reflect the point of view of the president, the president's family, and the president's institutional advocates."

I am ambling through the museum, past pictures of Nixon, all smiles in China, and one of the other visitors asks a guard,

"Where's Watergate?" The guard tells him, "Keep going straight. It's a dark room." And it is, a very dimly lit tunnel chronicling the break-in at the Watergate Hotel through President Nixon's resignation and farewell.

It does take you back. Have I mentioned that Nixon's face on television is my very first memory? Born in the first year of his administration, by the end of it, during the ever-present Watergate hearings on television, I thought *Watergate* was just a regular TV show, like *Bonanza* or *Scooby-Doo*. My mother claims it was unnerving to have a four-year-old always tugging at her hem saying, "Mom, Watergate's on!"

There are stations in the Watergate gallery where one may listen to the famous tapes, and there are intricate text panels with labels like "What Did the President Do and When Did He Do It." John Taylor says that one of the purposes of this exhibit is that people come here expecting the museum to avoid such a sore subject, and that dealing with it in such an info-packed manner gives them credibility.

According to Taylor, "The most important reason to tell the story is that it happened. It was an amazing outbreak of political passion. The anger that Congress expressed during the Senate investigation in 1973 and the impeachment investigation in 1974. It was passion that had been building probably since the events around the time of Kent State. I think one sees the same effect with President Clinton, who was also a figure about whom there were simmering passions among many conservatives. There was a strong feeling among many conservatives, as we all know, that he "was not legitimate." Or that he had been engaged in activities that had never been

27

fully revealed to the American people. And many of those passions came forth during the impeachment investigations and proceedings in 1998 and 1999."

Offering advice to you and your library director, President Clinton, Taylor says, "I think that it would be appropriate for the Clinton presidential library that there was a political dimension to the Clinton impeachment. And there were people who did not think President and Mrs. Clinton should be in the White House who used the impeachment effort as a way to accomplish that end. Pointing that out is fair comment. We point it out in our museum, and I would think and assume that they would attempt to do so in Little Rock as well."

In fact, Taylor says that one curious effect of the recent impeachment is the way it retroactively colors the Nixon legacy. Even if Nixon looks no better, his enemies don't seem quite as pure. Now, Taylor says, people are more likely to notice the vindictiveness and the sheer partisan glee that are bound to shadow any presidential impeachment.

There's a lot you can crib from the Nixon library, Mr. President. Just substitute the name Clinton for the name Nixon in the following text from the Watergate exhibit: "Nixon himself said he made inexcusable misjudgments during Watergate. But what is equally clear is that his opponents ruthlessly exploited those misjudgments as a way to further their own, purely political goals."

One caution, Mr. President: the Nixon library can sometimes seem a little defensive. In the LBJ library, a visitor's view of history is complicated by the presentation of both sides of the Vietnam dilemma. It's an emotional place, but it still oper-

ates within the language of good old-fashioned civics—a president and constituents loudly agreeing to disagree. The Nixon
library asks, You want facts? We'll give you some facts! And,
oh, by the way, grow up, because you're not going to like any of
them.

Recalling the Nixon library's exhibit marking an anniversary
of the deaths of four students at Kent State, Taylor asserts,
"Thanks to the Neil Young song, thanks to the way that event
is generally packaged in the media and in history, one rarely
hears about it from the perspective of Richard Nixon. But
when you hear President Nixon talking in our presidential forum about what a dark day that was for him, it challenges the
prevailing thought that he was callous and unfeeling towards
the families of those who had died. In fact, he says in this museum and says in his memoirs that it was the darkest day of his
presidency. And he includes Watergate when he makes that
calculation. At the same time, however, you also learn, when
going through the museum, that President Nixon had to weigh
the lives of those four innocent young people against the lives
of innumerable South Vietnamese and American soldiers
whose lives were saved as a result of the incursion of Cambo-
dia, which was the proximate cause of the demonstration at
Kent State, which got out of hand and led to the deaths."

President Clinton, perhaps you're wondering if the Nixon
library changed my mind about anything. You're wondering if
citizens who shook their fists at your face on TV might someday drop in on a building with your name on it and maybe give
you a break.

All I can tell you is that I still think Watergate's a horror and Vietnam was wrong. But I do find it useful to remember that those decisions, even the most deadly ones, were made not by a supernatural monster but by a real man whom we elected, a man who at least believed he was right. And that is not nothing.

In fact, the Nixon and Johnson libraries were my favorite ones to visit *because* they deal with quarrelsome subjects. Once, years ago, I was at the LBJ. I was walking away from a copy of the Voting Rights Act of 1965 toward a photo of a serviceman who had been killed in Vietnam. In the ten seconds it took to walk from that law to that face, a song from a nearby pop music exhibit started playing: "Louie Louie." And I felt like all of America was in that ten seconds: the grandeur of civil rights, the consequences of war, and the fun, fun, fun of a truly strange song.

Mr. President, Americans like contradictions. We elected you, didn't we? So in your library, own up to your failures, but don't stop trying to win us over. In other words, just think of it as running for president forever.

God Will Give You Blood to Drink
in a Souvenir Shot Glass

A few years ago, I was in Paris, taking a walking tour of the French Revolution, because that's how I spend my vacations. I also took another walking tour on the Fourth of July about Thomas Jefferson's Paris years, because I celebrate the Fourth of July—I do—but I take walking tours, I and the other retirees, because—I think I can bring myself to admit this—I am a *history buff*: I am one 1-800 number away from ordering the Time-Life World War II series off the TV. I have set my alarm so I wouldn't miss a C-Span morning live remote from the house of the Revolutionary War pamphleteer Thomas Paine. I celebrated my thirtieth birthday at Grant's tomb. My airport reading material—a novelization of Gettysburg here, a Lyndon Johnson biography there—always receives an approving glance from whatever middle-aged man on my flight is perusing the new Stephen Ambrose book, because every domestic flight requires a middle-aged man with a Stephen Ambrose book in his carry-on luggage—it's an FAA regulation.

When I was in Paris on the Thomas Jefferson walking tour, I learned that the core of the Library of Congress's book collection was purchased from Jefferson after theirs got burned down by those British bastards. Though I could be wrong about that, since a car was passing and I couldn't hear too well. Jefferson bought books every day in the bookstalls on the Seine, that I know, and, also, walked everywhere. Walked like a maniac apparently.

The French Revolution walking tour I took was mostly a drag, except for a gripping if questionable anecdote about Danton, whose lip was split when he was sucking milk from the teat of a cow and the bull came up and knocked him down and while he was lying there a bunch of pigs trampled his face. Nevertheless, according to the guide, an Englishwoman in a hat, the ladies adored Danton because he was "so vital."

But there was this one part, this breathtaking metaphorical jackpot, in which the Englishwoman led us down a cobblestone street, almost an alley, to the Rue St. Séverin. So we're in the Rue St. Séverin, which she points out by waving at one of those blue street signs attached to the buildings there. Then she points past the blue modern street sign to the place where "RUE SÉVERIN" had been carved into the masonry in the eighteenth century. In between the RUE and the SÉVERIN is this rough indention. A hole. Englishwoman, who heretofore hasn't been that dramatic, which is puzzling considering what's more dramatic than the French Revolution, what with the guillotines and let-them-eat-cake (brioche, actually, I was informed). She flourishes at the scratchy hole thing and says that the word *saint* was gouged out during the revolution because the revolutionaries were running around destroying references to the church and the monarchy. It was a big rut in the stone where the Christianity used to be. Have you ever heard of anything so beautiful or perfect? A better picture of history itself, a kind of erasing and revamping with fresh new signs hanging below the telltale gaping holes, holes made with meaning and purpose and no small amount of glee? Well, right before some nice old priest got his head lopped off, but still.

The historical periods I like to learn about aren't so much costume dramas as slasher flicks. The French Revolution is a favorite because it features the beloved plot of carnage in service of democracy, but I prefer American history. And if I had to pick my pet domestic bloodbaths, nothing beats Salem or Gettysburg. I'm a sucker for Puritan New England and the Civil War. Because those two subjects feature the central tension of American life, the conflict between freedom and community, between individual will and the public good. That is a fancy way of hinting that sometimes other people get on my nerves. I'm two parts loner and one part joiner, so I feel at home delving into the epic struggles for togetherness.

Plus, Puritanism and the War Between the States inspired some of the greatest American writing, scary sermons and Lincoln's speeches, writing which asks, to me, the question: If you're so gung ho on the fellowship of your countrymen, why have you had your phone off the hook for the last four days? I revere the idea of the Union, adore that phrase of Lincoln's when he asked the country to carry on "with malice toward none." And what of the prettiest Puritan sermon, the "city upon a hill" one John Winthrop delivered on a ship approaching Massachusetts in 1630? He aspired toward a covenant of community, decreeing, "We must delight in each other, make others' conditions our own, rejoice together, mourn together, labor and suffer together, always having before our eyes our commission and community in the work, our community as members of the same body." Are there any nobler words than that? And yet, did Winthrop ever live next door to a neighbor who was training a puppy? Would he have been so keen on us suffering together if he had just awoken to screams of "Naughty, naughty, no, no!"

The most bizarre episode in Puritan history is the Salem Witch Trials. Twenty innocent people were executed in Salem during the witchcraft hysteria of 1692. Which is horrifying, yet manages to make for a surprisingly nice weekend getaway. I went up one Saturday, ate dinner in sight of the Customs House where the Salem native Nathaniel Hawthorne began *The Scarlet Letter*, then got up for Sunday breakfast at the coffeehouse where the Sons of Liberty plotted the Revolution in 1776.

Salem boasts everything you would want from a trip down American memory lane, from information to anxious giggles. At the Witch Dungeon Museum, a place about as dignified as it sounds, there is the fun kind of bad actress in a period costume emoting through a reenactment of Elizabeth Proctor's witch trial, "I am not a witch! I am innocent!" There's a colorful old guy walking-tour guide named Bob who must not be a member of the chamber of commerce because he says things like "They hung dogs for being witches, that's how stupid these people were." There are freaky talking mannequins in the Salem Witch Museum that recite the Lord's Prayer and while they do resemble shrunken apples they nevertheless help the visitor understand how hard it must have been for the condemned to say the line about forgiving those who trespass against us. There's an old cemetery so archetypal it looks as though a child has drawn it as a decoration for Halloween. There is the seventeenth-century House of the Seven Gables that Hawthorne wrote about, where I decide to stop reading *The New York Times* "House & Home" section because, during the tour, the slave quarters strike me as really pretty. And there are a few yellowing historical documents to look at in the Peabody Essex Museum so that I don't feel like a total cheeseball, even though I just bought a whiskey glass emblazoned with a little yellow highway sign with a silhouette of a hag on a broomstick that says, "Witch XING."

On July 19, 1692, a woman named Sarah Good stood on the gallows and answered the minister making a last-ditch effort to get her to confess to witchcraft. She famously proclaimed, to the reverend and, I'm guessing, the town, "You are a liar; I am no more a witch than you are a wizard, and if you take away my life, God will give you blood to drink." Could she have any idea then that, three centuries later, bloodthirsty tourists would sip her life story from a souvenir shot glass? What would she think of the local ice cream parlor going by the name Dairy Witch? Or that the high school football team is called the Salem Witches? Or that a cartoonish witch logo adorns the town's police cars and newspaper? Or that the town that put her to death based on the harebrained testimony of a few teenage girls would remake itself as a vacation spot nick-named Witch City?

As Bob the tour guide said of Salem's witchcraft hysteria, "We're not ashamed of it." On the one hand, why not? It's a shameful episode. On the other hand, there are few creepier moments in cultural tourism than when a site tries to rewrite its past. Once, I took a boat tour up the Hudson and visited a seventeenth-century Dutch farm. At the farm there was a dif-ferent tour guide at each station—the bridge, the mill, the manor—and to a man (they were all women actually) they de-scribed the farm's slaves not as slaves but as "enslaved Afri-cans." As in "The mill was worked by enslaved Africans." Or "Over there were the cabins of the enslaved Africans." Or "That was the job of the enslaved Africans." After a while I couldn't stand it anymore and cornered one of these shawl-wearing tour guides and asked point-blank why on earth no-body used the word *slave*. And in that singsong dialect of teenage girls, in which every sentence ends in a question mark, she replied, "Because 'enslaved African' describes slav-ery as something that was done to them? Instead of what they were? Enslavement was not their whole identity?"

"Um," I asked, "isn't the whole point about being a slave that you don't have a choice to be anything else?" Prettying up the word *slave* with that adjective-noun construction makes "enslaved African" sound nonchalant. As in "Those were the cabins of the jolly leprechauns."

This isn't anything to be proud of. Those cringing, galling

moments are, for me, one of the big draws of visiting historic sites in the first place. I'll admit, one of my happiest moments in Salem was in a gift shop in which one of my fellow tourists asked the cashier if she was selling any "witchcraft trivets." To which the cashier replied, "You mean a trivet with a witch on it?"

On one level I understand that it is a disrespectful affront to the twenty people who lost their lives—including Giles Corey who was pressed to death—to such a grave injustice that this tourist wants to remember his visit to their hometown by purchasing an object to protect his dining room table from a boiling saucepan. At the time, that didn't stop me from enjoying a good chuckle at his expense. But once I returned home, I felt guilty.

I called my friend Kate, asking her if she could figure out why I do the things I do. Kate is a psychologist who counsels people with actual historical problems, like Kosovar refugees, at the Bellevue-NYU Program for Survivors of Torture. (If you really want to dampen your excitement about seeing the new Tom Hanks movie, just call Kate at her office to pick a show time and hear the receptionist answer the phone, "Program for Survivors of Torture.") Kate asked what was wrong, and I told her that I'd just gotten back from Salem and I had a really good time.

"Is that normal?" I wondered. "How come I never go to the Caribbean or Martha's Vineyard or someplace that's a travel magazine's idea of fun?" I told her how much I enjoyed the Rebecca Nurse Homestead near Salem. "Why should I want to spend my Saturday seeing the farm where a nice old lady who was hanged three hundred years ago used to live? I'm a pretty happy person. Why am I drawn to these gruesome places?"

"Well, it's not denial," Kate responds. "It's the opposite of denial. Something is playing out in your unconscious. Maybe you feel guilty about your happy life."

"But it's not like I'm going to Gettysburg or Salem just to earnestly mourn. I go there and joke around. When I had breakfast in Salem, I ordered bacon, the food of joy."

"So," she says, "you enact your ambivalence. You feel two ways about American history. Your life turned out great, but you're disgusted by the creepiness. So you take your own happy self to sites of disaster in order to deconstruct your ambivalence."

"Isn't that immoral?"

"No, that's how we try to make sense of the worst horrors. We use humor to manage anxiety."

Which got me thinking. I've been "managing" my "anxiety" pretty well lately. In fact, the last year has probably been the happiest of my life. So what does it mean that in the last twelve months I've taken trips to the sites of so many historical tragedies? Besides Gettysburg and Salem, I've dropped by Little Bighorn Battlefield (more ominous than Gettysburg in that a bunch of headstones mark the spot where soldiers in Custer's 7th Cavalry fell down and died); the North Dakota ranch where Theodore Roosevelt escaped when his wife and mother died on the same day; Dealey Plaza in Dallas; and the George W. Bush inauguration.

If I had to nail down the objective of my historical tourism, it's probably to collect evidence in support of my motto. And my motto in any situation is *"It Could Be Worse."* It could be worse is how I meet every setback. Though nothing all that bad has ever happened to me, every time I've had my heart broken or gotten fired or watched an audience member at one of my readings have a seizure as I stand at the podium trying not to cry, I remind myself that it could be worse. In my self-help universe, when things go wrong I whisper mantras to myself, mantras like "Andersonville" or "Texas School Book Depository." "Andersonville" is a code word for "You could be one of the prisoners of war dying of disease and malnutrition in the worst Confederate prison, so just calm down about the movie you wanted to go to being sold out." "Texas School Book Depository" means that having the delivery guy forget the guacamole isn't nearly as bad as being assassinated by Lee Harvey Oswald as the blood from your head stains your wife's pink suit. Though, ever since I went to Salem, I'm keen on "Gallows Hill." As in, Being stuck in the Boise airport for ten hours while getting hit on by a divorced man with "major financial problems" on his way to his twentieth high school reunion is irksome, but not as dire as swinging by the neck on Salem's Gallows Hill.

So if I have gleaned anything useful from reading and day-tripping through the tribulations of the long dead, it's to count my blessings, to try and quit bellyaching, buck up. Can't you just hear the children's song:

> *Gallows Hill and Andersonville*
> *It could be, could be worse*

Another reason I'm intrigued with the hanged of Salem, especially the women, is that a number of them aroused suspicion in the first place because they were financially independent, or sharp-tongued, or kept to themselves. In other words, they were killed off for living the same sort of life I live right now but with longer skirts and fewer cable channels.

On the first day of school when I was a kid, the guy teaching history—and it was almost always a guy, wearing a lot of brown—would cough up the pompous same old same old about how if we kids failed to learn the lessons of history then we would be doomed to repeat them. Which is true if you're one of the people who grow up to run things, but not as practical if your destiny is a nice small life. For example, thanks to my tenth-grade world history textbook's chapter on the Napoleonic Wars, I know not to invade Russia in the wintertime. This information would have been good for an I-told-you-so toast at Hitler's New Year's party in 1943, but for me, knowing not to trudge my troops through the snow to Moscow is not so handy day-to-day.

The other sort of useful thing the history teacher in the brown jacket never really said, probably because he would have been laughed out of the room, was this: knowing what happened when and where is fun. The next time I go to Paris, before I get my first croissant, I'm heading straight to that street and look for that hole. That hole was the best part of my trip. It's even more enjoyable to learn hole-like factoids about where you live, because you can see them all the time. Picking up my dry cleaning in my neighborhood, Chelsea, seems more festive since I found out that this is where Clement Clarke

Moore wrote "'Twas the Night Before Christmas." (Well, until some historian proved that Moore lied and stole the poem from someone else, but, hey, the plot thickens.)

The more history I learn, the more the world fills up with stories. Just the other day, I was in my neighborhood Starbucks, waiting for the post office to open. I was enjoying a chocolatey caffé mocha when it occurred to me that to drink a mocha is to gulp down the entire history of the New World. From the Spanish exportation of Aztec cacao, and the Dutch invention of the chemical process for making cocoa, on down to the capitalist empire of Hershey, PA, and the lifestyle marketing of Seattle's Starbucks, the modern mocha is a bittersweet concoction of imperialism, genocide, invention, and consumerism served with whipped cream on top. No wonder it costs so much. And, thanks to Sophie and Michael Coe's book *The True History of Chocolate,* I remembered that cacao beans were used as currency at the moment of European contact. When Christopher Columbus's son Ferdinand captured a Mayan canoe in 1503, he noticed that whenever one of the natives dropped a cacao bean, "they all stooped to pick it up, as if an eye had fallen." When you know such trivia, an act as mundane as having an overpriced breakfast drink becomes imbued with meaning, even poetry. Plus, I read a women's magazine article called "5 Fabulous Morning Rituals," and it said that after you "bask in bed" and "walk in nature" you're supposed to "ponder the sins of the conquistadors."

The New German Cinema

When I was growing up pretentious in Bozeman, Montana, I got all my ideas about going to the movies in New York City from the Woody Allen oeuvre. That's the word I would have used too, *oeuvre*. Because I was a teen cinéaste. These days, I'd describe myself as a moviegoer, but back then I was gaga for the *accent aigu*. In Woody Allen movies, people stood in line for Ingmar Bergman films or holocaust documentaries, talking up media theory to pass the time. At sixteen, that was my idea of fun. Now that I live in New York I can tell you that people lined up for tickets don't debate theory; they talk about cute guys at the gym or whether or not they live within walking distance of a Krispy Kreme.

I was such a young fogy that growing up involved becoming *less* mature. In my defense, I was a product of my environment. My hometown is a college town populated by a minority of city-slicker refugees who taught Western kids Western civ.

Marooned at cow college, these humanities types pined for pretense. So they organized a weekly film festival, slanted heavily toward foreign product. I remember one night so cold the cars wouldn't start, moviegoers sprinting in the forty-degrees-below-zero cold to watch something Danish. And I remember I once overheard a teenager telling her mother after the actually entertaining *Wings of Desire* that Wim Wenders had "sold out." See, we were mad for the New German Cinema, the sixties generation of filmmakers from West Germany who made gritty, questioning art in the shadow of their parents' Nazi barbarism. Like, people in Bozeman would do impressions of characters from Volker Schlöndorff films, walking up behind you and screaming at the top of their lungs, then asking, "Who am I? Who am I?" and you'd say, "Duh. Oskar from *The Tin Drum*."

The New German Cinema craze started in the mid-eighties, thanks to the head of the local college's film school. I took his class once. It was called something innocuous like Introduction to Cinema, so a lot of frat guys and cowboys signed up, thinking they'd fulfill humanities requirements by watching "movies." You should have seen the looks on their faces the day we saw the black-and-white film where a teenage girl gets her period on camera. Or the day we screened Rainer Werner Fassbinder's *Why Does Herr R. Run Amok?* In it, a humdrum businessman goes about his humdrum business—listening to his harpy wife, helping his son with his homework, talking to his visiting parents—for what seems like hours, until the last five minutes, when he goes berserk and bludgeons his family to death. Afterward, we were supposed to discuss existentialism. The professor asked if anyone had read Camus. I, of course, had read *L'Étranger* in the original French, and raised my hand. I mentioned the protagonist who doesn't care about his mother's death. Then I said that I often washed dishes with my mom. When she'd hand me a knife to dry, I would have the fleeting thought that it would be pretty easy to kill her if I wanted. I should mention that I usually sat in the back, so when I said this about a hundred heads whipped around to stare at me. What I should have said was, "But I don't want to kill her!" What I actually said was, "Oh, like you never thought about killing your mom." It was at that moment that I realized how small the New German Cinema community really was.

I have friends here in New York who occasionally invite me to some plotless downer at the Film Forum, but I always decline. They probably think I'm just some rube. But the truth is, I outgrew existentialism and subtitles. At some point in my mid-twenties I discovered fun. The only film by a German director I've seen since I moved here is Wolfgang Petersen's *The Perfect Storm*. But I earned the right to munch popcorn as the ocean messes up George Clooney's hair, because I sat through *The Bitter Tears of Petra von Kant*—twice.

Democracy and Things Like That

It all started in 1999, when Joanne McGlynn's media literacy class at Concord High School in Concord, New Hampshire, invited all the presidential candidates to speak. Known to loiter in New Hampshire ceaselessly before the state's primary elections, a whopping 50 percent of the eight major candidates accepted: Alan Keyes, Orrin Hatch, Gary Bauer, and Al Gore. They were asked to speak on the subject of school violence, not just because of the murders at Columbine earlier that year but also because a Concord High student was killed at school a couple of years earlier.

Gore spoke to the student body on November 30, 1999. And, contrary to conventional wisdom regarding his charisma deficiency, he was a hit. Students Lucas Gallo, Ashley Pettengill, and Alyssa Spellman recall the event.

Lucas claims, "He wasn't as stiff as people say he was. He

comes out, takes his jacket off. He walks around, talks to the audience."

Ashley remembers, "There was the question that said, 'What do you like to do for fun?' And he mentioned that he liked *The Simpsons*."

"He understood that we are people," Alyssa says. "We are kids but we're not dumb. We understand what's going on, and he respected that."

Lucas laughs, admitting, "He was still Gore. But he wasn't quite as stiff. He didn't just get up and talk like the other candidates did. He was kind of a neat speaker to see."

While the students were impressed by Gore's easygoing manner—his form—Joanne McGlynn was pleased with his content, the way he talked about school violence. "He was very careful to describe the complicated nature of what might have caused what happened at Columbine," she recalls. "He didn't say, 'It is just because those two boys played video games.' He used a little analogy about when you catch a cold or when you don't. He said that some kids in this auditorium had the insulation of a loving family, of teachers who cared about them, of a supportive school system and said perhaps they were insulated from some of these outside forces. And, therefore, were immune from committing those kinds of acts."

Then, during the question and answer period, something happened that seemed unremarkable at the time. A boy stood up and asked a mundane question about how high school students could become more involved in politics.

"He answered in a lengthy response," McGlynn recalls. "He thought for a moment, paused, and said, 'I know there's a lot of cynicism in the country right now, especially among young people. He said, 'I think it's caused by a number of things. Maybe we need campaign finance reform.' And he went on and talked about how he supported McCain-Feingold. He then said, 'But I think you kids should look in the mirror.'

"I think that leaders can make a difference," Gore told the student. "But I think you also have to examine your own hearts. We are so privileged to live in this country. If that sounds corny to you, you should examine that attitude. Seriously. Think about South Africa. They just recently became a democracy. When they had their first election, you know what the percentage turnout was? It was like 95 percent. People waited in lines to vote that were seven miles long. Here we have a constantly declining voter turnout. I think it's because a lot of people feel like they cannot make an individual difference. But you can."

McGlynn says, "So he challenged them to get involved, and then he said, 'Let me tell you a little story.'"

In the days that followed Gore's appearance, this little story was twisted, distorted and, ultimately, more fought over than a piece of Jerusalem real estate. And so I will quote his anecdote in its entirety:

> Let me tell you a quick story. Twenty years ago, I got a letter from a high school student in West Tennessee about how the water her family was drinking from a well tasted funny. She wrote me how her grandfather had a mysterious ailment that paralyzed part of his body, that she was convinced was related to the water. Then her father also

became mysteriously ill. People thought she was imagining things. We investigated, and what we found was that one mile from her home a chemical company had dug a big trench and they were dumping millions of gallons of hazardous chemical waste into the ground. It had seeped down into the water table and contaminated her family's well and the wells of other families in that rural area. I called for a congressional investigation and a hearing. I looked around the country for other sites like that. I found a little place in upstate New York called Love Canal. I had the first hearing on that issue and Toone, Tennessee—that was the one you didn't hear of. But that was the one that started it all. We passed a major national law to clean up hazardous dump sites. And we had new efforts to stop the practices that ended up poisoning water around the country. We've still got work to do. But we made a huge difference. And it all happened because one high school student got involved.

The night after the speech, Joanne McGlynn's at home, and a friend calls her, asking if she's seen *The New York Times*. "He said, 'Did you notice the Love Canal comment?' And I said, 'I remember he told a story about Love Canal.' And he said, 'The *Times* says that Gore's taking credit for finding Love Canal.' And I thought, Uh-oh. I got a bit nervous. I thought, Is that the way this story is going to be covered?"

The *New York Times* article in question, by Katherine Seelye, ran on December 1, 1999. In a seventeen-paragraph piece about one day in the Gore campaign, four paragraphs are devoted to the Concord High appearance. Seelye quoted Gore, "'I found a little place in upstate New York called Love Canal. I had the first hearing on that issue and Toone, Tennessee,' he said. 'But I was the one that started it all.'" It is curious that *The Washington Post* made the exact same mistake. Also on December 1, the *Post* staff writer Ceci Connolly quoted, "'I was the one that started it all.'"

Alyssa recalls, "We came into class and Ms. McGlynn was like, 'You guys are not going to believe this.' And she wrote the quote up on the board and she said, 'Did he say this?' and we were like 'What? What?' 'Did he say this: I was the one that started it all.' Then we were like, No, he was talking about the girl. That event started it all. And then we looked at all the newspapers and we were like, Wow."

Ashley: "She then played us back the tape that our TV production class had made and the actual quote was 'that was the one that started it all,' referring to the city in Tennessee."

According to Alyssa, "We definitely said we have to do something about this. And we were definitely I think shocked that, that one little word, *one little word*, totally changed the context and totally changed what everyone thought about it."

After the *Times,* and the *Post,* the Love Canal mistake snowballed. *U.S. News & World Report* listed "I was the one that started it all" as one of its quotes of the week. There was the following little roundtable about Gore and Love Canal on ABC's *This Week with Sam Donaldson and Cokie Roberts,* among the two hosts, George Stephanopoulos and Bill Kristol.

"Gore again revealed his Pinocchio problem," quips Stephanopoulos. "He says he was the model for *Love Story,* created the Internet, and this time he sort of discovered Love Canal. It was a kind of exaggeration."

"He said," says Roberts, "that he discovered Love Canal when he had hearings on it after people had been evacuated."

Kristol, reading from a paper that is presumably either the *Post* or the *Times,* says, "Yeah, 'I found a little place in upstate New York called Love Canal. I was the one that started it all.' "

Then *The Late Show with David Letterman* dreamed up a list of "The Top Ten Other Achievements Also Claimed by Al Gore." "Number 5," Letterman announces, "Pulled U.S. out of early '90s recession by personally buying 6,000 T-shirts.

> NUMBER 4: Started CBS situation comedy with Juan Valdez titled "Juan for Al, Al for Juan."
> NUMBER 3: Was inspiration for Ozzy Osbourne song "Crazy Train."
> NUMBER 2: Came up with popular catchphrase "Don't go there, girlfriend."
> And the number one other achievement claimed by Al Gore: Gave mankind fire!

Initially, the students at Concord High were upset about the misquote. But the more they thought about it, and the more they watched the misquote evolve, they were really flabbergasted by the misrepresentation of Gore's appearance at their school. Alyssa complains, "He was trying to say that kids can make a difference. He was trying to say what so many high school kids in this country don't believe."

Lucas understands that Gore was "running for president, so

he has to be a bit selfish and kind of boost himself when he's speaking, but the message—they totally missed the point of the entire story that he told. He was trying to make it a clear point for us that we need to get involved and that we should. And that we can do something to help. And the media didn't even mention the message he was trying to explain or anything."

Ashley thinks, "The actual quote itself was, I think, completely innocent. It wasn't a 'look how great I am, look what I did in Love Canal' it was a 'look how great you can be.' That's what his message was, and that's what the papers overlooked."

I played devil's advocate with Ashley, asking her, So what? The reporters got one word wrong but they got the gist of what Gore was saying right. What would she say to that?

She replied, "I would say, 'You're wrong.' You're focusing on one little itty-bitty microscopic thing that when misquoted can mean something completely different but when quoted correctly it means a great thing for democracy and things like that."

If I can come clean on whom I identify with the most in this story, it isn't the students or their teacher. I identify with the *New York Times* reporter Katherine Seelye, who misheard a word. *She* was the one that started it all. I am convinced that this woman, whose job it is to follow around a man with two jobs—running for president and being vice president—is beyond overworked. I know this partly because the first chance she got to return my phone call about all of this was at 1:15 in the morning. This poor reporter, this gatekeeper of democracy, was getting her first break in the day in the middle of the night.

And, considering that I am a writer who has publicly misspelled names, confused Sinclair Lewis with Upton Sinclair, and gotten who knows how many things wrong over the years, I am one pot who should not be calling the Gray Lady black. Both *The New York Times* and *The Washington Post* did publish corrections. And this is what Seelye told me. About the students of Concord High, she said, "These kids are well-intentioned. They're paying attention. We did get one word wrong. But they are magnifying what happened. Gore did say, 'I found a little town in upstate New York called Love Canal.' He called the AP in Buffalo the next day and apologized for presuming to take credit for that."

The journalists were in fact correct when they said that Love Canal was already a front-page story, an official national emergency, months before Al Gore ever held hearings. But Gore never claimed to have been the one to have first brought Love Canal to national attention. He only claimed to have held the first congressional hearings on it, which he did, after receiving that letter from Toone in 1978.

In the end, it's possible that the main difference between the ways the reporters and the class heard Gore's speech is that the reporters were listening for some new sound bite from Gore they hadn't heard before, whereas the students were listening for Gore's thoughts on school violence, an issue that is of grave concern to them, an issue Gore actually addressed. Their teacher Joanne McGlynn points out, "I think what shocks me though is that there seems, on some parts of the media that we've talked to, very little remorse. That surprises me. That it was just a word. I guess I have my own bias or per-

ception as I look at the event. The week before Al Gore came,
our entire school had to practice a lockdown procedure. And a
lockdown procedure is something that I had never experi-
enced except as a kid in Catholic school in Rhode Island in the
early sixties. The nuns had us hiding under our desks or
putting our heads down to protect us from nuclear fallout for
when the Russians were going to bomb us. And in 1999 we
were being asked to run through an event as though a sniper
were out in the hallway. This came down as a recommendation
from the state of New Hampshire, their safety planning group,
and it just so happened that we had our first practice session
the week before Al Gore came to Concord High School. So
our principal came over the intercom and said, 'Teachers,
please implement the lockdown procedure.' We knew ahead of
time this was going to happen sometime during the next two
days. I had to take my freshmen and move them away from the
door, get them on the floor, turn their desks on their sides so
they would be protected as much as they could be in case
someone came into the room or attempted to come into the
room with a gun. We had to be silent. I had to go out in the
hallway and lock the door and grab any kid who might have
been returning from the bathroom, hoping this kid was not the
person we needed to worry about, grab that kid, pull him in,
and ask my students to be quiet. I have to tell you, it was very
unsettling. The thought that one of ours, one of our students
could be out in the hallway trying to harm us—it's a very complicated emotional response. Many of us were very uncomfortable during the lockdown. But we couldn't show that to
the kids, wanted to show the kids that they were safe and not

to worry. So, I thought Gore did a good job talking about this issue. I thought this issue should be one of the prime ones in our presidential campaign, and I feared immediately when I heard Love Canal that, somehow, what had happened at Concord High would become a joke. And, in some ways, that is what happened."

On his talk show *Hardball,* Chris Matthews chuckled. "Let's talk about Al Gore and have some fun. We've gone from the serious part of the program, now here's the hilarious part. Al Gore keeps taking a little bit of truth and building it up into this epochal role in history."

Joanne sighs. "It just makes me sad that the wise-guy attitude seems to dominate the press right now. That's what I pick up on. Not to pick on Chris Matthews, but he spent two nights having a blast with this story about Love Canal. Getting a big chuckle out of 'Dan Quayle may not be able to spell *potato* but now Al Gore's going to claim he invented it.' Well, maybe where Chris works that seems like a funny thing to say, but where I work, it didn't seem that funny. Where I work, pretending to be hiding behind desks with kids, afraid that Klebold and Harris are outside my door, it didn't seem that funny. And I'm not saying our candidates should be untested, unquestioned, uncriticized. What I am saying, if that's all we do, and if all we do is make fun of them, then we're losing something too, I think."

Ashley tells me, "I feel like some reporters are just saying what [the candidates] did wrong." When I ask the sixteen-year-old what we lose when the press omits descriptions of how a candidate might actually make a good president, she answers, "I think we miss out on every reason to vote for them."

At Concord High School, a politician actually spoke inspiringly and connected with the audience. Which, to me, *is* news. But no reporter reported this. And in fact these kinds of moments are routinely overlooked by the press. They're barely part of our national political discourse. But why? For one thing, so much political speech is lies, spin, and misrepresentation, it's understandable that journalists report these inspiring moments skeptically, if at all. And, beyond that, the way most of the press works is pretty much as you suspect; representatives of the news media carry around story lines of the candidates in their heads, and reporters light up when reality randomly corroborates these pictures.

One of the great mysteries of modern politics is which story lines get told and which get ignored. And, in the primary season, that story line is still up for grabs. John McCain's story line—hero—threatened to become "hypocrite" in light of his helping a major donor with the FCC. Not long after George W. Bush flunked a foreign policy pop quiz, his name tag at the correspondents' dinner was destined to read, "Hello, my name is Dunderhead." Gore's story line—that he's a bore—is spiced up by this secondary story line: that he's a braggart, that he takes credit for ridiculous things, for inventing the Internet and for being the real-life Oliver of *Love Story.* So of course the Love Canal misunderstanding screamed to reporters because it brought this particular fuzzy snapshot of Gore into sharper focus.

It is telling that both the reporter for the *Times* and the one for the *Post* heard the exact same word incorrectly, almost as if that was what they wanted to hear. Joanne McGlynn says that this is a seductive impulse for both reporters and voters. She says, "This editor for *U.S. News & World Report* called and said that; this was after he admitted that he was sorry they had published a misquote. He told me a story about George Bush, Sr., running for president in 1992. And I remember the story myself that George Bush went into a supermarket and was stunned to find a scanner. I guess he was used to old cash registers and made a comment that showed he was surprised to see a scanner. What this gentleman from *U.S. News & World Report* told me was, actually, the pool reporter got that story wrong, that it was actually some kind of *new* scanner that Bush remarked on. But that comment then became the iconic moment for Bush being out of touch with Middle America. And that was it. I think that might have hurt Bush big time. Now, it turned out—if this man from *U.S. News & World Report* is right—not to be accurate. Now, if it wasn't accurate, was it not true? I mean, was Bush out of touch with Middle America? It's the same thing going back to Gore: Does Gore take credit? It makes me question. And I have to say, I am going to keep my eyes open in a way I hadn't before, particularly when things automatically fit my mind-set. I'm going to be a little careful. It didn't surprise me that maybe President Bush didn't know about a scanner. But if he did, it's too bad that got out there. It's not fair."

I looked at Joanne McGlynn's syllabus for her media studies course, the one she handed out at the beginning of the year, stating the goals of the class. By the end of the year, she hoped her students would be better able to challenge everything from novels to newscasts, that they would come to identify just who is telling a story and how that person's point of view affects the story being told. I'm going to go out on a limb here and say that this lesson has been learned. In fact, just recently, a student came up to McGlynn and told her something all teachers dream of hearing. The girl told the teacher that she was listening to the radio, singing along with her favorite song, and halfway through the sing-along she stopped and asked herself, "What am I singing? What do these words mean? What are they trying to tell me?" And then, this young citizen of the republic jokingly complained, "I can't even turn on the radio without thinking anymore."

Pop-A-Shot

Along with voting, jury duty, and paying taxes, goofing off is one of the central obligations of American citizenship. So when my friends Joel and Stephen and I play hooky from our jobs in the middle of the afternoon to play Pop-A-Shot in a room full of children, I like to think we are not procrastinators; we are patriots pursuing happiness.

Pop-A-Shot is not a video game. It involves shooting real, if miniature, basketballs for forty seconds. It's embarrassing how giddy the three of us get when it's our turn to put money into the machine. (Often, we have to stand behind some six-year-old girl who bogarts the game and whose father keeps dropping in quarters even though the kid makes only about 4 points if she's lucky and we are forced to glare at the back of her pigtailed head, waiting just long enough to start questioning our adulthood and how by the time our parents were our age they were beholden to mortgages and PTA meetings and here we are, stuck in an episode of *Friends*.)

Finally it's my turn. A wave of balls slide toward me and I shoot, making my first basket. I'm good at this. I'm not great. The machine I usually play on has a high score of 72, and my highest score is 56. But considering that I am five foot four, that I used to get C's in gym, and that I campaigned for Dukakis, the fact that I am capable of scoring 56 points in forty seconds is a source of no small amount of pride. Plus, even though these modern men won't admit it, it really bugs Joel and Steve to get topped by a girl.

There are two reasons I can shoot a basketball: black-eyed peas and Uncle Hoy. I was a forward on my elementary school team. This was in Oklahoma, back when girls played half-court basketball, which meant I never crossed over to the other team's side, which meant all I ever had to do was shoot, a bonus considering that I cannot run, pass, or dribble. Blessed with one solitary athletic skill, I was going to make the most of it. I shot baskets in the backyard every night after dinner. We lived out in the country, and my backboard was nailed to an oak tree that grew on top of a hill. If I missed a shot, the ball would roll downhill into the drainage ditch for the kitchen sink, a muddy rivulet flecked with corn and black-eyed peas. So if the ball bounced willy-nilly off the rim, I had to run after it, retrieve it from the gross black-eyed pea mud, then hose it off. So I learned not to miss.

My mother's brother, Hoy, was a girls' basketball coach. Once he saw I had a knack for shooting, he used to drill me on free throws, standing under the hoop at my grandmother's house, where he himself learned to play. And Hoy, who was also a math teacher—he had gone to college on a dual math-basketball scholarship—revered the geometrical arc of the swish. Hoy hated the backboard, and thought players who used it to make anything other than layups lacked elegance. And so, if I made a free throw that bounced off the backboard before gliding through the basket, he'd yell, "Doesn't count." Sometimes, trash-talking at Pop-A-Shot, I bark that at Joel and Stephen when they score their messy bank shots. "Doesn't count!" The electronic scoreboard, unfortunately, makes no distinction for grace and beauty.

I watch the NBA. I lived in Chicago during the heyday of the Bulls. And I have noticed that in, as I like to call it, the moving-around-basketball, the players spend the whole game trying to shoot. There's all that wasted running and throwing and falling down on cameramen in between baskets. But Pop-A-Shot is basketball concentrate. I've made 56 points in forty seconds. Michael Jordan never did that. When Michael Jordan would make even 40 points in a game it was the lead in the eleven o'clock news. It takes a couple of hours to play a moving-around-basketball game. Pop-A-Shot distills this down to less than a minute. It is the crack cocaine of basketball. I can make twenty-eight baskets at a rate of less than two seconds per.

Joel, an excellent shot, also appreciates this about Pop-A-Shot. He likes the way it feels, but he's embarrassed by how it sounds stupid when he describes it to other people. (He spent part of last year working in Canada, and I think it rubbed off on him, diminishing his innate American ability to celebrate the civic virtue of idiocy.) Joel plays in a fairly serious adult basketball league in New York. One night, he left Stephen and me in the arcade and rushed off to a—this hurt my feelings— "real" game. That night, he missed a foul shot by two feet and made the mistake of admitting to the other players that his arms were tired from throwing miniature balls at a shortened hoop all afternoon. They laughed and laughed. "In the second overtime," Joel told me, "when the opposing team fouled me with four seconds left and gave me the opportunity to shoot from the line for the game, they looked mighty smug as they took their positions along the key. Oh, Pop-A-Shot guy, I could hear them thinking to their smug selves. He'll never make a foul shot. He plays baby games. Wa-wa-wa, little Pop-A-Shot baby, would you like a zwieback biscuit? But you know what? I made those shots, and those sons of bitches had to wipe their smug grins off their smug faces and go home thinking that maybe Pop-A-Shot wasn't just a baby game after all."

I think Pop-A-Shot's a baby game. That's why I love it. Unlike the game of basketball itself, Pop-A-Shot has no standard socially redeeming value whatsoever. Pop-A-Shot is not about teamwork or getting along or working together. Pop-A-Shot is not about getting exercise or fresh air. It takes place in fluorescent-lit bowling alleys or darkened bars. It costs money. At the end of a game, one does not swig Gatorade. One sips bourbon or margaritas or munches cupcakes. Unless one is playing the Super Shot version at the ESPN Zone in Times Square, in which case, one orders the greatest appetizer ever invented on this continent—a plate of cheeseburgers.

In other words, Pop-A-Shot has no point at all. And that, for me, is the point. My life is full of points—the deadlines and bills and recycling and phone calls. I have come to appreciate, to depend on, this one dumb-ass little passion. Because every time a basketball slides off my fingertips and drops perfectly, flawlessly, into that hole, well, swish, happiness found.

California as an Island

Noticing an Audubon ornithological engraving in the hall of a stranger's apartment, I found myself humming the opening bars of Nirvana's "Lithium" and craving a burrito. Audubon's birds take me back to a specific time and place—not the eastern backwoods of the 1820s but San Francisco when I was twenty-four. As a teen beatnik, I had dreamed of growing up and joining some Bay Area subculture. I just imagined my subculture would have a little more razzle-dazzle than the demimonde of antiquarian prints and maps. But managing a gallery owned by a notorious dealer named Graham Arader was the only job I could get, and I was grateful for it. Before he hired me, I had been temping for months, spending entire days inserting plastic tabs into file folders or begging the Chinese callers to the Chinese television station to please speak English as the Chinese receptionist is taking a personal day.

It occurs to me now how preposterous it was that a girl who

lived on a foldout couch in her married friends' living room for a year was having a say in the decoration of swank Pacific Heights mansions. At the Arader Gallery, I hung gigantic Audubon pelicans and delicate little eighteenth-century prints of lilies and roses on the wall, wrote gushy letters to collectors about four-hundred-year-old maps of North America, and helped the sales staff try to peddle chromolithographs of the Grand Canyon to walk-ins. I boned up on natural history, discovering that the Carolina parakeet Audubon painted is now extinct, and that once upon a time there were buffalo in Poland. Some days I felt like a contestant in a cartography game show, as I rushed to research a map in three minutes if a salesperson had a live one. For shipping, I learned how to construct a cardboard box of any shape and size. I answered the phone. I fetched coffee. I made sure we didn't run out of Bubble Wrap. At the end of the day, I would set the gallery's alarm, put very loud grunge music on my Walkman, take the slow bus home, and pull another graduate school rejection letter out of the mailbox. Then my friends and I would drink some bottle of wine they learned about on their doomed Napa honeymoon until it was time for me to unfold my crummy foldout couch. They would be divorced by the end of the year, and it occurs to me now that having an interloper camped out on their sofa for thirteen lucky months could not have helped.

I was miserable, but I had been miserable before. All three years of junior high school spring to mind. But I had never had the privilege of unhappiness in Happy Valley. California is about the good life. So a bad life there seems so much worse than a bad life anywhere else. Quality is an obsession there—

good food, good wine, good movies, music, weather, cars. Those sound like the right things to shoot for, but the never-ending quality quest is a lot of pressure when you're uncertain and disorganized and, not least, broker than broke. Some afternoons a person just wants to rent *Die Hard,* close the curtains, and have Cheerios for lunch.

I remember how at home I felt, the first time I left. The gallery sent me east to learn from the master at Graham Arader's Pennsylvania headquarters. Getting off the plane from San Francisco at the Philadelphia airport, I was taken aback. I realized I had been living under quarantine in some euthanized, J. Crew catalog parallel universe of healthy good looks. Because, in Philadelphia, I was pleasantly surprised to see old people, average people, even ugly people, ambling around in dumb T-shirts and home perms. And if that wasn't relief enough, the weather was terrible and the coffee was dreck. The nice thing about Philadelphia is that no one has moved there to find the good life for over two hundred years. I went home to California feeling like the prettiest, most upbeat over-achiever in the world.

For as long as I can remember, one thing that has always lifted my spirits is research. (In San Francisco, that sentence is supposed to end on the words "sailing," "gay sex," or "driving down to Carmel for the weekend.") I find looking things up consoling. And of all the collections I had to research in my job at the gallery, I became enamored of a period in European cartography in which California was depicted as an island. The gallery had quite a few of these maps, published in the seventeenth and eighteenth centuries in Paris, London, and

Amsterdam. I hung them so I could see them from my desk. The idea of California as an island was a lie and a myth, but from where I was sitting, it seemed true enough. The gallery's girl Friday, I was stranded on it. There might as well have been a little red arrow pointing at every one of those Californias next to the words "You Are Here."

The consensus on what happened with the California-as-an-island maps was that Dutch pirates seized a Spanish boat containing an erroneous map or journal describing California as an island and in 1622 Dutch map publishers started to update their charts accordingly. Then the Londoner Henry Briggs jumped on the bandwagon in 1625. Though two of the great Dutch publishers, Jodocus Hondius and Willem Blaeu, refused to buy into the fad, the error was reprinted in many European maps well into the next century. California is an island, for example, on the map illustrating Daniel Defoe's sequel to *Robinson Crusoe* in 1719. It was a Jesuit, Father Eusebio Kino, who set out to put an end to the rumor, which makes sense considering the missionaries were the biggest victims of the false information, dragging boats they didn't need halfway to Cleveland. Kino made a map in 1701 confirming that California was attached to the mainland, and the mistake was fixed for good in 1747, when Ferdinand VI of Spain issued a royal decree proclaiming, "California is not an island."

Clients always wanted to talk about the California maps. Maybe it was because we were in California or maybe it was because the maps were so mysterious or because everyone likes to point out how stupid people used to be. Or maybe they were dying to make one of the fourteen San Andreas Fault "not an island . . . yet!" jokes I heard every week.

Even though the salespeople and I would chat up the California maps with customers all the time, every day, I don't recall that we ever sold a single one. Which makes sense considering that of Graham Arader's five galleries around the country, we made the least money, and don't think the boss didn't notice. We were the worst map sales force of all time working for the greatest map salesman in history.

Arader was the kind of fascinating boss about whom employees gossip with a mix of adulation and dread—one of those go, go, go guys whose ambition you could admire while at the same time hoping you weren't the one who answered the phone when he called. Under my breath I called him the Grahamarader, because I thought of him as an action-movie killing machine, like Arnold Schwarzenegger in the Terminator movies.

It makes sense to me now that Graham's life's work involves the buying and selling of maps and natural histories from the Age of Discovery, when ambitious, even godlike men lit out to see and document and tame the flora and fauna of the New World. Graham's beginnings in the early 1970s sound so American, so go-west-young-man. The guy was dealing maps out of his dorm room at Yale. His mother ruined his first big sale. Chagrined, he recalls, "What happened was, I'd been working the whole summer buying maps of Penobscot Bay for Thomas Watson, who was then the chairman and chief operating officer of IBM. He had never met me. I had met him by phone. I went ahead and found all these fabulous maps that showed Penobscot Bay. So at the end of the summer I'd amassed this really incredible collection. I was living with my parents at the time. I was twenty-three years old. And when Mr. Watson called, not knowing who he was or why he was calling, my mother said, 'I'm sorry, you'll have to use the children's phone.' Mr. Watson hung up and didn't talk to me again for two years."

My favorite legend about the Grahamarader, one printed in *The New Yorker*, so presumably it may even be true, is that Graham once desired a map owned by a friend. Graham begged the man for it. Graham told the man that he needed the map, that he loved this map so much he wanted to hang it over his bed, that it would be the first thing that he saw when he got up in the morning and the last thing he saw when he went to sleep at night, that he wanted to conceive his children under it. The friend was so touched he sold the map to the Grahamarader, who promptly called the friend the very next day bragging that he'd sold it, and for a tidy profit at that.

Map dealers, I came to learn, are not like that. As a group, they tend to be polite, bookish, and don't inspire comparisons to Schwarzenegger or any other mythic pop figure. Graham is the map dealers' Michael Milken, their Elvis Presley. In financial terms, he put antiquarian maps on the map. And he popularized them like no one ever had through sheer charisma. "The antiquarian map market before Graham Arader," says Graham, "was a fairly sophisticated market. The people who collected had in-depth knowledge and understanding. I guess the effect that I had is that I brought map collecting to a lot more people who perhaps in the beginning were not as sophisticated. And the prices have gone up and I get blamed a lot."

In other words, he functions as the messiah of the map biz, or its Antichrist, depending on your point of view. The entire industry can be divided B.A., Before Arader, when many historical maps sold for a few hundred dollars, and A.A., after Arader, when the same maps began commanding tens of thousands of dollars.

One by-product of Graham's excitement and salesmanship is hyperbole. He carries around a small but well-used toolbox of superlatives, which he hammers into everything, words like *Fabulous!* and *Greatest!* and his favorite, *Best!* I think he formed the hyperbole habit by saying things like "John James Audubon is simply the finest bird painter who ever lived!" Perusing his catalogs, one learns that the engravings based on the Swiss painter Karl Bodmer's *Travels in the Interior of North America* are "the most detailed study of the Plains Indians ever produced"; that George Catlin's Indian lithographs are "one of the finest portrayals of Plains Indian life ever created"; and that Currier and Ives were responsible for "the most popular and highly regarded lithographs of quintessentially American scenes ever produced." Maybe Graham always talked like that. Somehow, I can picture a five-year-old Graham telling his mother, "Mom, these are absolutely the greatest oatmeal scotchies ever baked in North America!"

Graham Arader sells history. He's a passionate historian. He probably knows as much about the history of cartography as any academic on the planet. It's what he does with all the information in his head that always astonished me. Graham's inventory encompasses the sixteenth through nineteenth centuries. Think about those dates. Think about the story being told in European and American maps of that era. Dutch maps of South Africa. French maps of New France. It is not just one story but two—a great adventure of nation building and the promise of the New World, but also one of theft and warfare and genocide. Guess which one of those stories sells maps?

Watching him sell something is fun. It is exciting. It is patriotically inspiring. He showed me a map of America, cooing, "This . . . map . . . tells the story of Manifest Dessssssss-ssssstiny!" And I'm thinking, Yeah! Manifest Destiny! Wow! What a country! Then I catch myself, remembering, Oh yeah, Manifest Destiny. In fact, once, at the San Francisco gallery, a client walked in looking for Manifest Destiny memorabilia. I opened a drawer and pulled out a print copied from John Gast's famous painting *American Progress*. In that picture, Columbia, the barely dressed mythological female representation of America, floats west over the prairie, stringing telegraph wire as a train, stagecoach, and various settlers also head to the Pacific beneath her. The man couldn't have been more pleased, swooning over the little covered wagon, the little farmer plowing, the Brooklyn Bridge near the eastern edge, the quivering Indians looking over their shoulders in fear. He was smiling as I took his credit card, told me he was going to hang it over his breakfast table. Personally, I wouldn't want to look at those shivering Indians as I munched my corn flakes. Why wake up to original sin? The only picture I can see from my breakfast table is a strategically placed snapshot of my baby nephew taking a nap with a puppy.

In his Manhattan gallery, I once watched Graham show a sixteenth-century book to one his favorite clients. The book was filled with beautiful engravings depicting the natives of the English colonies. "So this was the beginning," Graham says. "This volume was from the voyage that John White took in 1585, and it was published in Frankfurt in 1590, and it really is the first image that Europeans had of the Cherokees, Creeks, Seminoles, Choctaws." He turns a page, pointing. "That's how they had smoked alligator and lizard. Here's how they caught the deer. Look at that. That's cool."

And it is cool. It's a lovely book. It is exciting to see the first image of the Cherokees. But the other voice in my head keeps saying, "Trail of Tears, Trail of Tears, Trail of Tears." There's something aesthetically pleasing about trading one engraving—an old map—for another—American money. What could be more perfect than someone paying for that book with all the Cherokees with a big fat roll of twenty-dollar bills, exchanging the graven images of Andrew Jackson, Mr. Trail of Tears himself, for the story of the tribe he sought to destroy?

The hardest part about working around all those ambiguous American artifacts was biting my tongue. I would be showing a client an early map of South Carolina, and he would be looking for his hometown or talking about color and out loud I would say, "Hmm, delightful," but my brain would be droning, "Slave state." I couldn't believe someone would want to hang that on his wall, though now that I think about it, the man probably looks at that map all the time and the only thing it reminds him of is how he really should call his mom.

I could have filled a history book with things I couldn't say to the buyers. I couldn't tell the bird-watcher beaming at Audubon that Audubon had to shoot a lot of those birds to paint them. Or tell the couple admiring the Bodmer lithograph of the Mandan ceremonial dog dancer that the guy in the picture was probably dead soon after he posed because smallpox wiped out 90 percent of his tribe. Or tell the fellow spending all afternoon deciding whether or not to buy Catlin's buffalo hunt picture for his office that in Catlin's first letter about the natives he was drawing he wrote that the "means of their death and destruction have been introduced and visited upon them by acquisitive white men." Can I wrap that up for you, sir?

Graham Arader's America is a prettier picture than mine. And he believes in it. That is why, as he would say, he is the best, the finest, the most successful antiquarian map dealer in the history of the world. His is an easier picture to sell. But it's also a lovelier, less sarcastic one to buy. I want to buy it. I like the telegraph and the railroad and the Brooklyn Bridge. Graham's map of America has an elementary school quality that I admire. How many times have I wished to go back there, to live once more in the country I thought I lived in as I stood on the stage of the second-grade Thanksgiving pageant, singing "This Land Is Your Land" in a cardboard turkey suit?

I think the reason I wasn't cut out to be a good map seller or a good Californian had something to do with the fact that I dressed up as Wednesday Addams for Halloween that year.

The Addams Family and *The Munsters,* shows where roses were grown for their thorns and pretty blondes were pitied as monsters, were on TV every afternoon after school when I was a little kid. Throw in three Pentecostal church services a week where they preached that the Antichrist would be a sunny, smooth, all-American charmer, and you have the makings of an insular worldview. Namely, a sneaking suspicion that there's always a dark side of nice.

When I called Graham those years ago to tell him I was quitting my job and leaving California to go to Chicago to study art history, he told me what a dumb idea that was and how I would learn a lot more about art by selling it. At the time, I laughed. But I can see now what he meant. There's something educational about trying to see the good in things, holding some old picture in your hands and telling another person why it's significant and excellent, special.

Dear Dead Congressman

A rosy letter about voting written the day before an election day now infamous for poorly designed butterfly ballots, disenfranchisement of black voters, nationwide malfunction of voting machines, incompetent network TV coverage, and a snippy Hillary Clinton campaign worker insulting me as I walked into my polling place to vote for her candidate:

November 6, 2000

Dear Congressman Synar,

I've never written to a dead man before. But there's something I always meant to tell you, and I'm not going to let a little fatal cancer stop me. You probably won't remember me. My mother used to do your mother's hair in Muskogee in the sixties. My parents still have one of her paintings, by the way, a brownish still life with flowers. When you were running for the House that first time, in 1978, I handed out some pamphlets for you at my town's rodeo. I'm from Braggs. I was eight. I live in New York City now, and it's been a long time since I've been to a rodeo in Oklahoma (or anywhere else). At the Braggs rodeo, you shook my hand and gave me the "Synar for Congress" button off your own lapel—which I still have—and told me it was the last one off the printing presses. You'd think Elvis was handing me his sweaty scarf or something, I was so excited. I realize now how young you were. You were twenty-seven then, younger than I am now.

There's this letter you sent me right after your election. I've kept it with me all these years. It's written on House of Representatives letterhead marked "Mike Synar, Member-Elect, 2nd District, Oklahoma." It reads:

> Sarah—
> Thank you so much for your help during our campaign. Don't forget that when you become eighteen you should get registered to vote. Get involved in government and our government will be better.
> Thank you again Sarah
> Best Wishes,
> Mike Synar

Lord knows, you probably mailed hundreds of these notes during your sixteen years in the House. It's even possible an aide wrote it, but in my heart of hearts I believe it came from your own pen. I must have pulled it out of the envelope and reread it a thousand times, dreaming. Someday, I thought.

How I pined to vote. In 1985, the movie *The Breakfast Club* came out. In my teen world, it was a really big deal. Every kid who saw it was supposed to identify with one of the stereotype characters—the rebel, the weird girl, the jock, the nerd, the princess. I identified with Anthony Michael Hall's nerd, Brian. (Though I was only about nine months away from turning into black-clad, antisocial Ally Sheedy.) There was this one scene, my favorite, in which Ally Sheedy has just stolen Anthony Michael Hall's wallet. Jock Emilio Estevez is looking at the nerd Hall's phony driver's license, pointing out that it says the nerd, who looks like he's twelve, is sixty-eight years old. Clearly, the kid's no barfly, so the jock's suspicious.

JOCK: What do you need a fake ID for?
NERD: So I can vote.

I cast my first vote in 1988, in the Montana Democratic primary, for Jesse Jackson. I handed out pamphlets for him too—hope you don't mind that I started seeing other candidates. My love for Jackson was pure, was unconditional and real. I rode my bike eight miles on a highway shoulder, swerving around roadkill, to hear him speak at the airport.

As you know, he lost. I'm sure you can relate. (Sorry about '94, by the way. Some tough year for Democrats, especially those who campaigned so hard for the president. When your friend Bill Clinton delivered your eulogy in 1996, he said this about you, "When he was defeated in 1994, there was probably no person in America more responsible for it than me.")

It's that time again. On Tuesday, I'll be going over to the

housing project on Twenty-fourth Street to vote. I think of you every time I draw the voting booth curtain behind me, every time I pull the lever. I love it in there. I drag it out, leisurely punching the names I want as if sipping whiskey in front of a fire. I mean, how many times in a life does an average person get to make history?

I sometimes look at the appendix in an American history reference book I have that lists the vital statistics of all the presidential elections. For example, during Andrew Jackson's successful reelection campaign of 1832, William Wirt of the Anti-Masonic Party garnered 101,051 votes. Eight percent of the voters went for Wirt, and I like to think that if you put the chart under a microscope, you can see all their rotting white male faces crammed inside that number, chanting, "Not him! Him!"

On Monday, September 25, I was watching the David Letterman show and something happened I'll remember for the rest of my life. The day before, the Sunday *New York Times* magazine ran a story about how television comics are influencing the coming election. The article quoted a former Letterman writer who called Letterman a "non-voting Republican." To me, that phrase stuck out, for three reasons. The first reason is that I am extremely partisan, a capital *D* Democrat, and I'm always on the lookout for which of my heroes might be Republican. (Though I would say of Letterman what I always say about Frank Sinatra—his work doesn't make you *feel* like a Republican.) Second, as a regular Letterman viewer, I knew that earlier this year he was called for jury duty in Connecticut because he talked about jury duty every damn night for weeks.

And how do you get called for jury duty? By registering to vote. So "non-voting Republican" sounded fishy, but scoffing at the *New York Times*'s mistakes is a morning ritual, like oatmeal. Finally, the phrase "non-voting Republican" stuck out because that is how one might describe Dick Cheney, who responded to press attacks that he didn't vote in local elections by saying he was more focused on "global concerns." Which I think is a polite way of saying he was out of town on the corporate payroll sticking it to foreigners and couldn't be bothered with what his running mate might rhapsodize as "local control."

Anyway, Letterman. I wish you could have seen him. This presidential election has been so weirdly down-to-earth, so issue-oriented, that Letterman's tirade was maybe the only moment of true over-the-top grandeur of the whole campaign. Letterman brought up the *Times* magazine article, said it was about political humor, and stated that it characterized him as a non-voting Republican. "When I heard this," he said, "frankly, I was insulted." He recalled voting in 1968: "That was my first election. We had an ugly, awful war going on. It's not an election about who's banging interns." He mentioned he also voted in 1972 and then spent the rest of the seventies abstaining, because those were his "cocktail waitress days." For this he was embarrassed, confessing, "I realize that that was an irresponsible way to live. I straightened myself up. I come here, I'm living in New Canaan, Connecticut, so I registered to vote." To corroborate this, he called up the registrar of voters in New Canaan, a man named George, who confirmed that Letterman has voted in every election since at least 1988. "Prior to 1988, they don't know," Letterman continued, because previous records are kept in a vault somewhere and "they're scared. They don't want to go down there." He laid out his evidence as though testifying, concluding, "So I think I've established, Your Honor, I do vote."

I don't know if I'm capturing the intensity of this, of the sheer civic thrill of watching someone so clearly offended by being called a nonvoter, as if *nonvoter* is some kind of curse word, a slanderous insult he couldn't not refute. His outrage was so—there's no other word for it—righteous. I was touched. The litany closed like an old-fashioned oration. Thus saith the talk show host, "I believe I have voted for both Democrats and Republicans. Am I either one? Absolutely not. Ladies and gentlemen, I am an American." At which point, I, in my living room, clapped.

One of the items on the Green Party candidate Ralph Nader's platform is election day voter registration. Theoretically, I support anything that increases voter turnout. On the other hand, what's easier than filling out a card with your address on it four weeks before the election? Christ, this thing's been going on for over a year now. Who are these lazy idiots who can't pay attention more than five minutes before they cast their votes? Isn't voting called *suffrage,* a word that sounds like doing it should hurt a little?

Speaking of suffrage, I'll end this on the following thought. The protagonist in a recent movie called *The Contender,* about the confirmation hearings of a vice presidential replacement, admits that she's an atheist but says that she has a religion. Her faith is the idea of American democracy itself. It's what she believes, believes *in.* I was struck by that, because that's how I feel too. During the New Hampshire primary I got in a screaming fight with the candidate Gary Bauer. Okay, I screamed, he didn't. He had just whipped a little paperback copy of the Declaration of Independence and Constitution out of his pocket and said that anyone who doesn't believe in God, doesn't believe in those documents because of the phrase "endowed by their Creator." I told him that, on the contrary, those documents for me have superseded God, that they are my Bible.

All of which is to say, look up the word *suffrage* in the dictionary. In mine, after noting the main meanings—the privilege of voting, the "exercise of such a right," the third interpretation of suffrage is this: "A short intercessory prayer." Isn't that beautiful? And true? For what is voting if not a kind of prayer, and what are prayers if not declarations of hope and desire?

I guess I'll end my letter to you the way you ended yours to me.

Thank you again Mike.

Best wishes,

Sarah Vowell

The Nerd Voice

PART ONE   The Nerd Israel

In the movie *Revenge of the Nerds III: The Next Generation,* Harold, the nephew of the hero from the first film in the series, arrives at his uncle's alma mater, Adams College. Thanks to Uncle Lewis's crusade for nerd rights, the previously jock-ruled campus has now turned the gym into a computer science center. There are cheerleaders, but these cheerleaders chant, "E! Equals! M! C! Squared!" Harold tells his friend, "Adams College is one of the first schools in the country to treat nerds with respect. It's the Promised Land. Kind of like a nerd Israel."

Ever since I started opening my morning e-mail to find two or ten or twenty postings from an e-mail group devoted to tracking the 2000 presidential election, that's how I have come to regard the Internet. The Internet is the nerd Israel, a place to speak and listen to spectacularly specific concerns. According to a sex advice columnist I know, whenever he receives a letter from a lonely fetishist who wants to get in touch with others who, say, also enjoy biting the heads off of dolls, all my friend has to do to cheer up the advice seeker is type the words "biting off doll heads" into a search engine and have five Web links to other doll head biters appear straightaway.

The inherent specificity of the Internet made it the perfect forum in which to discuss the 2000 presidential campaign and postelection bedlam. From Bush and Gore haggling over pennies for senior citizens' prescription drug costs before the election to Bush and Gore haggling over a few hundred votes in the state of Florida after the election, it was a year of minutiae. So what better way to evaluate those events than poring over statistics with your egghead friends? Especially Paul, our doting numbers cruncher. Interpreting polling data about the public's perception of the legitimacy of Bush's presidency, he wrote, "So assuming that those 39 percent of respondents all voted against him, that means that of the 53 percent of Americans who opposed him, three-quarters believe that he stole the election, and that his presidency is illegitimate." I have no idea if that's true because I'm not sure what it means.

The political e-mail group might be the all-time nerdiest thing I've been involved in, and I say that as a person who has been involved in public radio and marching band. All of us were Al Gore supporters of varying levels of enthusiasm— a bunch of nerds rooting for a nerd. Joel, a group member from Brooklyn, describes it as "this weird bastion of totally out of touch liberalism." A typical message about a group member's Saturday night begins, "Late Saturday evening, I finished reading about Inauguration Day in *The Washington Post* and the *L.A. Times* and ABC News on-line and MSNBC on-line. . . ."

A few of us went down to Washington to watch the inauguration. Jack, a Connecticut father of two, drove down in his titanic dad van, setting off from his house in New Haven, picking up Deirdre and Paul in Milford, and stopping for Kevin and me in New York. We're all friends, but this trip isn't an act of friendship so much as the culmination of a laborious process.

On the eve of our road trip to the inauguration, I wasn't sure I was going. It promised to be depressing. The forecast called for rain. But Kevin's e-mail convinced me. A novelist given to grandiose electronic orations, Kevin is the group's dinosaur, an old-school, Roosevelt-style Democrat out of fashion enough to go on and on about the fate of the poor, the unlucky, and the young. His e-mails are grand WPA murals commemorating the ordinary yearning to live and work in an honest, earthy republic. More than anyone I know, Kevin would make the best president. At the same time, he's the least electable. He's the biggest hothead in the group, which is saying something. We are not subtle people.

Kevin implores us to drive down to the inauguration "to be able to say to those of our children's grandchildren's generation that at least we were not willing to let American democracy—to let America—die without standing up and being counted." No pressure. He continues, "This is the real crucible of being a true American now—to stand up for what we believe in without illusions, without any real hope that we will be able to change anything. There will be no great, new third party to rescue us; no grassroots revival of the Democratic Party. All there is—is us, willing to stand up and say no."

He actually talks like that. In January 2001, it was hard to be a patriot without sounding like a conspiracy theorist.

Before joining the e-mail group, I had always thought of citizenship as a duty. For the group, citizenship became a sort of hobby. Some days it was a part-time job. The discussion of current events would follow some historical tangent, such as whether or not the early Clinton administration should have honored the promised middle-class tax cut instead of going for deficit reduction in 1993, and we would bicker about the findings of former Labor Secretary Robert Reich and blah, blah, Alan Greenspan, and the next morning I would wake up to find that in the middle of the night my friend Stephen had called me a "deficit hawk," which, in his vocabulary is a synonym for "Republican."

The best part about being a nerd within a community of nerds is the insularity—it's cozy, familial, come as you are. In a discussion board on the Web site Slashdot.org about *Rushmore,* a film with a nerdy teen protagonist, one anonymous participant pinpointed the value of taking part in detail-oriented zealotry:

> Geeks tend to be focused on very narrow fields of endeavor. The modern geek has been generally dismissed by society because their passions are viewed as trivial by

those people who "see the big picture." Geeks understand that the big picture is pixilated and their high level
of contribution in small areas grows the picture. They
don't need to see what everyone else is doing to make
their part better.

Being a nerd, which is to say going too far and caring too
much about a subject, is the best way to make friends I know.
For me, the spark that turns an acquaintance into a friend has
usually been kindled by some shared enthusiasm like detective
novels or Ulysses S. Grant. As a kid, I never knew what to say
to anyone. It was only as a teenage musician that I improved
my people chops. I learned how to talk to others by talking
about music. At fifteen, I couldn't say two words about the
weather or how I was doing, but I could come up with a para-
graph or two about the album *Charlie Parker with Strings*. In
high school, I made the first real friends I ever had because
one of them came up to me at lunch and started talking about
the Cure.

I have fond feelings for the people in the e-mail group. "A
nice sense of community during wartime," the low-key Paul
says about the group's exchanges during the postelection period of vote-counting-in-which-votes-weren't-counted. Kevin
amps up Paul's wartime comparison by identifying with the
Free French circa 1940, calling us "rudderless, leaderless, confused, and bitter." While I find it flattering that Kevin would
equate our computerized griping with battling Nazi collabora-
tors, I don't really feel like the French Resistance for two rea-

sons—they looked cool and, with a soupçon of help, they prevailed.

Campaign 2000 was what a mail-order catalog might call a real conversation piece. Thanks to the Internet and the twenty-four-hour news channels, the kind of inside-the-Beltway chat that used to be quarantined in the Sunday morning network TV talk shows is everywhere, all the time. It's Sunday morning every day. The political class has had this freakish population boom, as though that bitch George Will gave birth to a litter of bow-tied puppies and they all found homes. And all the commentators and columnists and party flacks and talk show hosts are hustling and spinning as much as, if not more than, the politicians themselves. For me, the novelty of the e-mail group was simply finding out what a relatively average, intelligent, home-owning, middle-class father like Jack thought about tax policy or campaign tactics. Our e-mails were different than just talking around a dinner table: We were a sort of homegrown talk show, where one person would state an opinion and then everyone else would go McLaughlin Group on his ass.

Looking back, it's stunning how much of the political group's e-mail was fueled by powerlessness. Especially during the up-in-the-air gray area between the election and the Supreme Court ruling that decided the winner. There was nothing we could do but come together and type loud.

Sending messages to the group "did change the way I followed things," Stephen tells me. "Or not so much changed it as focused it. It was more fun coming on some info knowing you'd get to pass it on to someone like-minded. There seems to be no end to the satisfaction one gets in having one's opinions confirmed."

For instance, inauguration day coverage, a topic we scrutinized even more than usual because we were actually there. We'd been part of an uneasy national event. We had noticed plenty of jolly celebrants, but we'd been elbow to elbow with scores of enraged, sign-toting protesters too, one of whom—an acquaintance of Kevin's—held up a sign directed at Bush that simply said, "I Hate You." So the next morning's press postmortem in the group was particularly thorough. Paul's posting about the lead stories on the inauguration in *The Washington Post* and *The New York Times* shows how a typical reader of one or the other—a regular person who does not belong to a sarcastic Internet consortium of amateur media watchdogs—would have formed entirely different opinions of the event's, for lack of a better word, vibe. Paul remarks that *The Washington Post*'s fifth paragraph mentions "thousand of sign-waving protestors" but complains that the *Times*'s lead story finally mentions the protesters in paragraph forty-nine, but that "there is no further word on who those protesters might be, how many of them there were, or what they might have been protesting." Stephen forwards a London *Observer* piece that reads, "The *Observer* considers [Bush's] election an affront to the democratic principle with incalculable consequences for America and the world."

Walking to the inauguration, we duck into the National Archives to look at the Declaration of Independence and the

Constitution, just to see if they're still there. Jack chats with the guard about the nuclear-proof underground vault the documents are lowered into every night. Then it's on to the police checkpoint. The inaugural parade route is completely blocked off, and the only way in is through checkpoints where the authorities search all bags. It's all over the news that, thanks to the healthy number of expected protesters, they've banned fruit, as well as sticks attached to protest signs. Also, giant puppets. Those things could be used to hit another person. Never mind that my club-shaped umbrella is admitted without a word, or that a president endorsed by the NRA is so apparently worried that a cantaloupe or marionette might put out some spoilsport picketer's eye. The police search of my backpack is anticlimactic, no big deal. I was actually hoping for a little more cop interaction, because I thought it would be amusing if I had to account for the Abraham Lincoln paper dolls I'm carrying in my backpack that Jack bought at the archives for his two little girls. Maybe the cop and I would even share a brief but lighthearted moment of communion, agreeing that Mary Todd Lincoln sure had dumb hair. The cops must be humoring us to check our bags, as we are the least threatening-looking group of people here. Even elderly Republican ladies are more menacing than we are, because they have the guts to wrap themselves in controversial mink pelts.

We get to the muddy Mall just as Chief Justice William Rehnquist is swearing in Dick Cheney as vice president. From where we stand, the men are faraway specks. But, thanks to the CNN JumboTron, their faces are bigger than the Capitol dome. Rehnquist, as one of the five Supreme Court justices who effectively gave Bush the presidency, was a particular object of the group's e-mail scorn. We all boo him. Then we boo Dick Cheney. Or rather, I would like to think that it's nothing personal, that we are booing the fishy process that got him here. Staff Sergeant Alec T. Maly of the United States Army Band sings "My Country 'Tis of Thee." I'm stunned when Kevin boos him too. I ask him, "You're booing the army guy? You're booing 'My Country 'Tis of Thee'? Are we against everything now?" Yes, he answers, we're against everything, and boos louder.

George W. Bush places his hand on the same Bible that George Washington placed his hand on in 1789 and repeats after Rehnquist that he will "to the best of my ability, preserve, protect, and defend the Constitution of the United States." I'm sure he means it, if he's actually thinking about it, but it's reassuring to have that underground vault at the National Archives as a backup.

I told myself I came down to "protest." But I choose to display my dissent by bursting into tears as Bush finishes up his oath. Alas, my tears are my picket sign.

It's happened. It's over. He's it.

Once, I was prepared for this, even looking forward to it. Because before I am a Democratic nerd, I am a civics nerd first and last. Back before election day, there was a part of me—the part of myself I don't like—that harbored a secret, perverse desire that Bush would defeat Gore. Because a Bush victory, I thought, would offer me four illustrious years of taking the high road. I would be dignified. I would be wise. Unlike my Republican brethren, who pooh-poohed Bill Clinton's legitimacy from the get-go—Texas Congressman Dick Armey, speaking to Democratic colleagues, referred to him as "your" president—I would be a bigger person. During the Clinton era, being a civics nerd of any political stripe was like having the school bully paste a "Kick Me" sign on your back every day year after year. In my preelection daydream of what a Bush presidency might be like, I imagined that I would criticize his policies and lambaste his statements with a civic-minded nobility. All my venom, spite, and, as long as we're dreaming, impeccable logic, would be directed at *our* president. As in "Look how *our* president is wrecking *our* country."

Making my pompous little fantasy come true, however, hinged on one thing—a majority of people voting for Bush. Not only did he lose the popular vote by more than half a million ballots but he essentially won the electoral college by a single vote—that of the fifth Supreme Court justice who decided to halt the Florida recounts. So now what?

The CNN camera pans around the dais. Seeing Bush embrace his ex-president father, seeing him shaking the now ex-president Clinton's hand, seeing Gore clapping like a sad, good sport, all makes me cry harder. About the only person up there I find myself happy to look at is the former Republican senator and presidential candidate Bob Dole. I've developed a soft spot for Dole because he symbolizes a simpler, more innocent time in America when you could lose the presidential election and, like, not actually become the president.

Once he's back home in his apartment, Kevin sends an e-mail to those in our group who didn't come with us, describing what being on the Mall was like:

> Nearby, a pro-Bush family prayed with their heads down, holding hands, while the chaplains gave the invocation and the blessing. I found myself looking down, too, at all the mud on the Mall, and thinking about how young the country was. This was, after all, the primeval mud of our soggy capital, sunk into a Maryland swamp that everyone—diplomats, presidents, congressmen—used to complain about in the early decades of Washington's existence. There were plans in the mid-nineteenth century to really landscape the Mall—to turn it into some ingeniously planned English-style facsimile of nature, much like Central Park. But the landscape architect they hired died in a spectacular steamboat crash on the Hudson, and they never did get around to putting his plan in place. Instead, the Mall remains an intriguingly blank, muddy expanse, a sort of parade ground of democracy, and we all just stood out there to hear the speech.

The colossal head of Bush—*President* Bush—delivers his Inaugural Address on the JumboTron. It is not terrible. I find myself begrudgingly agreeing with most of it, though it will be weeks before I feel adult enough to admit that out loud. He says that the story of America is "the story of a slave-holding society that became a servant of freedom." I can't stomach unquestioning jingoism today, so I'm relieved that he refers to the slaves. That's where my head's at right now—that mentioning the slaves would cheer me up. It's a reminder that, hey, we enslaved people, we deserve to have this guy be our president.

This part of Bush's speech isn't bad:

> While many of our citizens prosper, others doubt the promise, even the justice, of our own country. The ambitions of some Americans are limited by failing schools and hidden prejudice and the circumstances of their birth. And sometimes our differences run so deep, it seems we share a continent, but not a country.

That line about not sharing a country is about the only time Bush even halfway alludes to the warring throng before him. After he finishes, Jack and I will trudge to the Lincoln Memorial to read the Second Inaugural Address carved into the wall. Bush thinks he's got problems? In his speech of March 4, 1865, Lincoln asked his countrymen "to bind up the nation's wounds." He recapped the still raging Civil War in point-blank terms, as if to say, "Don't think I haven't noticed how much we loathe each other." The speech's bravery derives from its very honesty. I think it's a mistake that Bush doesn't similarly come clean. How many furious citizens might have given him the benefit of the doubt if he just said that he sees us, if he just buttered us up a little, pronouncing that he knows he didn't get our votes but he will try to earn our trust? Well, Kevin wouldn't have bought it, but the rest of us suckers might have cut the new president some slack for a day or two.

PART TWO Nerds v. Jocks

On inauguration day, when Jack and I were walking down the Mall toward the Lincoln Memorial, past all the giggling Republican faces, it felt like being stuck inside the cover of that old Frank Sinatra album *No One Cares*. It's the one where there's a party going on and all the partygoers are smiling and dressed up and dancing, but Sinatra sits all alone at the bar, sighing into his whiskey glass. He has his coat on and he looks like he's remembering better times.

I was once a Washington intern, back when being a Washington intern was a goody-goody, model-citizen thing for a young lady to do. It was during the Clinton administration's bubbly first year. I moved into my new Adams-Morgan apartment the night before Yitzhak Rabin shook Yasir Arafat's hand for the first time on the White House lawn. I thought I could feel the world being saved a few Metro stops away. Looking at all the gleeful partisans on Bush's inauguration day took me back, that feeling of, Washington is ours! Oh, how my friends and I once cooed with excitement in the fall of '93 when we were seated at brunch a couple of tables over from George Stephanopoulos. All the other nubile New Democrats were smitten with George, though I myself had a little crush on the sad-eyed economic adviser Robert Rubin.

I had looked forward to Gore's Washington. With Gore running the country, it would be different. I would feel even more at home. Clinton had appealed to the rock 'n' roller in me, the part of me that went to Graceland and cried when Kurt

Cobain died and thinks about James Brown's hair. But Gore appeals to the real me, the one who can still sing a song from college German class about which prepositions to use with the accusative case—*"Durch, für, gegen, ohne, um: Akkusativ."*

Gore's pencil neck tugs at my nerdy soul. I think the most lovable thing he has ever said can be found in a sentence in his 1992 book *Earth in the Balance: Ecology and the Human Spirit.* On page 67, he asks, "What happened to the climate in Yucatán around 950?" Something about the specifics of that query lit me up. For the first time, I could see casting my ballot for a man who would pose such a question. It was just so boldly arcane. The kind of mind that would wonder about temperature variations on a Caribbean peninsula a thousand years ago might have the stomach to look into any number of Americans' peculiar concerns. Paradoxically, this fervor for scientific facts—the thing that alienates him from voters because they see him as cold—requires no small amount of passion. You don't write a four-hundred-page book about ecology unless you have the heart.

Of course, Gore being Gore, he doesn't write just about what he knows. Gore being Gore, he is compelled to confess the dweebish details of how he learned what he knows. *Earth in the Balance* features countless hints that his life is an ongoing study hall: "Since that time, I have watched the Mauna Loa reports every year" or "Beginning in January 1981, I spent many hours each week for more than thirteen months intensively studying the nuclear arms race." *January* 1981 he says—I bet it was his New Year's resolution. Every other member of

Congress was vowing to cut back on the hookers, but then-Senator Gore probably French-kissed Tipper at midnight and made a mental pledge to really get a handle on those ICBMs.

This is the Gore of the first presidential debate with Bush, the sighing, eye-rolling, eager beaver, buttinsky Gore, interrupting Bush to ask the moderator, Jim Lehrer, "Can I have the last word on this?" Ross G. Brown commented in the *Los Angeles Times*, "Gore studied hard and was thoroughly prepared for the televised civics and government quizzes each debate provided. A teacher might have given him an A. But much of the rest of the class just wanted to punch Mr. Smarty-Pants in the nose."

"I didn't think of Gore this way," my friend Doug told me on the phone one day, "but he was widely perceived as arrogant. If you know something, you're not smart. You're a smarty-pants. It's annoying. People get annoyed with knowledge. It goes back to high school, to not doing your homework. Everyone knows what that's like. 'Time to hand in your assignments.' And that dread of 'Oh, shit, I didn't do my assignment.' It calls that back. It's this feeling of 'There's something I should know. I don't know why I should know it but someone knows it and I don't. So I'm going to have to make fun of him now.' "

Before and after the election, I found myself having versions of this conversation again and again. "One of the frustrations about Al Gore," explained my friend John not long after the election, "is that he's uniquely qualified to be president by having the actual equivalent of street knowledge. He knows how the system works. I remember seeing an interview with

him on TV, it might have been a *Nova* episode on global warming in the mid-eighties. It was basically the first time I had ever
heard of global warming. And Gore was the young senator
from Tennessee. He very articulately explained what politics
is. Politics is people worrying about next year and right now.
The problem you have when the more you know about global
warming as a politician is the more you realize you can't do
anything with it. Experts bombard you with cold, hard facts
about what's going to happen fifteen years from now. You look
at your children. You know they're going to be living in that
world. You can see the train coming down the track. Gore said
one of the most frustrating things is that you can't run on that
because the public is not interested in wisdom and the public
is not wise. The public is actually reactive. So unless you can
create it as a scenario that's going to work for them right now,
it's just something you have to do behind the scenes. You have
to figure out how to sell your idea to people within the system.
And I just thought that's the most thoughtful assessment of
the nature of that kind of political problem. He was a young
guy. He was really casual and super savvy about it. I just
thought, Wow, that guy should be president! Later on, this
election, he couldn't even be who he was. He couldn't say, 'I
know a lot about this shit!' Because you can't say that you
know a lot about something or people will think you're uppity."

This is the subtext of the Gore campaign's press coverage.
Writing about a man who knows so much and who isn't shy
about sharing his knowledge must have gotten on a lot of jour-
nalistic nerves. Recalling Gore's press conferences, Eric Poo-

ley of *Time* wrote, "Whenever Gore came on too strong, the room erupted in a collective jeer, like a gang of 15-year-old Heathers cutting down some helpless nerd." Right after the election, a search on the Nexis journalism database for the following terms revealed these results. For "Al Gore and nerd," 804 articles. For "Al Gore and geek," 826 articles. For "Al Gore and dork," 136. For "Al Gore and Poindexter," 110. For "Al Gore and homework," 966. Searches for "George W. Bush and" the words *dumb, stupid,* and *idiot* were unable to be completed because those queries "will return more than 1,000 documents." All of which was distilled perfectly in the election day headline in the London *Daily Mail,* "The Nerd Versus the Nincompoop."

To be clear, I believe Al Gore technically won the 2000 presidential election. What baffles me is how close an election it was considering the simple, gaping chasm between the two candidates' qualifications. Compare their résumés. Gore served in the Congress, as both a representative and a senator, for sixteen years. As vice president, he helped mastermind the country's most successful economic expansion. He is an expert on environmental issues, foreign policy, military technology, and the digital communications industry. Before Bush was a two-term governor, he was a late-blooming, failed oilman who lucked out owning a baseball team.

In the televised presidential debates, Bush did well enough on general questions from his platform, but on a complicated question about what the United States should do if ousted Serbian President Milosevic refused to leave office, Bush said he would ask the Russians to lead the charge. Vice President Gore replied,

> Now I understand what the governor has said about asking the Russians to be involved, and under some circumstances that might be a good idea. But being as they have not yet been willing to recognize Kostunica as the lawful winner of the election, I'm not sure that it's right for us to invite the president of Russia to mediate this dispute there because we might not like the result that comes out of that. They currently favor going forward with a runoff election. I think that's the wrong thing. I think the governor's instinct is not necessarily bad because we have worked with the Russians in a constructive way in Kosovo, for example, to end the conflict there. But I think we need to be very careful in the present situation before we invite the Russians to play the lead role in mediating.

> BUSH: Well, obviously we wouldn't use the Russians if they didn't agree with our answer, Mr. Vice President.
> GORE: Well, they don't.

I don't understand why Gore didn't secure a landslide right then and there. On knowledge alone, it was a no-brainer. So why couldn't Gore carry his own home state of Tennessee, much less sweep the rest of the country? Clearly, it has something to do with who he is as a person, and who he is as a person is a big honking nerd. Nobody minds this in a vice pres-

THE PARTLY CLOUDY PATRIOT

ident. The vice presidency is actually a nerd's perfect job. A sidekick is supposed to be a bigger geek than the star. Like in the teen TV drama *My So-Called Life,* when the dreamboat boy Jordan Catalano gets the telephone number of a girl he doesn't know in two seconds flat, the nerd Brian Krakow asks him, "This is, like, how you live?" How many times Gore must have wanted to ask that question of Clinton, with the sidekick's tone of disdain mixed with awe.

The one time I ever saw Al Gore in person was during the 2000 primary. I attended his performance of Aaron Copland's *Lincoln Portrait* with the American Symphony Orchestra at Lincoln Center's Avery Fisher Hall. Gore narrated Copland's piece, which sets Lincoln's writings to orchestral accompaniment. It is possible that easily a third of the audience was there to have some fun at Gore's expense. But there was something quaintly reassuring about the way the crowd clapped—some even stood—out of respect for his office, which, lest we forget, is only respect for the electorate and its judgment. Even in cool New York, Americans are not above a little "He's here!" excitement, even over the then–vice president, a man who once joked about himself that Al Gore is so boring his Secret Service name is Al Gore.

The *Lincoln Portrait* has a long instrumental introduction, which provided ample opportunity to watch Gore wait and wait and wait for his turn to speak. It was like watching the institution of the vice presidency in action. This must be what it's been like for him all these patient years, listening to someone else's noise until it's finally his cue.

Gore, who sat in profile next to the conductor, Leon Botstein, looked like the head on a coin. Which is to say he never looked more presidential. It's an easy trick to come off dignified while wearing a nice blue suit in front of tuxedo-clad violinists and orating the words of Lincoln. Then again, orating the words of Lincoln is itself a gamble. Who could begin to compare? The music on the stage wasn't coming from the woodwinds. It was coming from the page, from the grave, from the rhythm of "new birth of freedom" and the melody that "we cannot escape history." Hearing words like that spoken by a presidential candidate was especially striking in the primary season. The practicality of the campaigners, Gore included, was mind numbing. They seemed to think of the American people as a bunch of penny-pinching misers who hoard their precious votes for the candidate who might save us forty bucks a year on the 1040EZ.

I was delighted to take a brief, poetic break from the tax breaks to sit there in Lincoln Center and ask, What is a president supposed to say? What should he sound like? Should he sound like Lincoln? We think we think so, forgetting Lincoln's actual voice, which was reportedly about as squeaky as a six-year-old girl's. Because his words were so eloquent, we imagine he had the stentorian boom of Gregory Peck. He did not. I personally suspect that Abraham Lincoln sounded exactly like me. Stereotypes die hard, and Americans have a deep desire for their president to sound, look, and act "presidential," which is to say flawless, verging on bland.

In Al Gore's first presidential run, in 1988, he knew so much about the greenhouse effect that one of his opponents accused him of "running for national scientist." But in the beginning of

George W. Bush's term, I couldn't help but wonder if he were running for national gym teacher. He should just go through life with a whistle around his neck. A couple of weeks into his administration, a gunman from Indiana took a shot at the White House. However, Bush was not in danger, because the would-be assassin assumed Bush was working in the middle of the workday. Bush was in the gym of the White House residence, exercising.

I immediately turned on CNN and started calling Stephen from the e-mail group, gurgling updates into the phone: Someone's shooting at his office but he's okay because he's somewhere else on the StairMaster! Then, on March 30, 2001, the Associated Press reported, "Creating his own field of dreams, President Bush pledged Friday to help revitalize interest in the national pastime with regular T-ball games on the White House South Lawn. 'We've got a pretty good-size backyard here,' said the baseball team owner turned president."

Kevin's e-mail: "Maybe, if we're lucky, W. will also plant a cornfield out by the outfield of his new White House diamond. Then maybe the ghosts of William Howard Taft and Grover Cleveland will emerge and fall on him."

If *Newsweek*'s Jonathan Alter is correct, Bush's jockish disdain for highbrow thought is the very origin of his White House bid. "In a 1998 *New Yorker* piece [about Al Gore]," Alter claims, "the vice president talked about the ideas of Maurice Merleau-Ponty, a French existentialist. Bush read the article, and later told friends it was one of the reasons he ran for president—to keep intellectual pretentiousness out of the White House." In his campaign, Bush promised to restore honor and

dignity to the White House, but the promise to keep intellectual pretentiousness out is one that is likely to be kept. I think
the happiest moment of Bush's presidency was the day he
hosted his first T-ball game. According to *The New York Times*,
"Mr. Bush laughed and laughed, and seemed particularly
amused by the antics of a man in a furry chicken suit who put
one baseball down the mouth of his costume and then
dropped two from the rear."

Adolescent nerds across the country must be shuddering
now that a jock is in charge of the dreaded President's Physical
Fitness Exam. Anyone who thinks the president has no effect
on an average person's life should corner a teenage girl and ask
her about the "flexed arm hang." I mentioned the President's
Physical Fitness Exams to Kevin and, after supplying historical context—"Actually, you have Jack Kennedy to blame for
them, who first publicized them with the help of the comic
book Superman"—Kevin admitted, "The real humiliation for
me was pull-ups. I could not for the life of me manage to pull
my (then) seventy-pound body up over that bar, and instead
would end up hanging there, grunting pitifully."

My friend Doug, like most nerds, never got over high
school. His nerd cred includes being able to name every Best
Picture Oscar winner since 1950 off the top of his head, as well
as maintaining a terrifyingly detailed recall of specific issues of
X-Men comics. Doug is a writer and producer for the television program *Buffy the Vampire Slayer*. *Buffy*, aside from being
the smartest, funniest, most consistently pleasurable drama
on television, uses nerds and explores nerdiness in a way that
is both intricate and appealing. I bring it up because Al Gore

could have learned something about being a public nerd from watching this show. If only he had ditched the professional politicos who fumbled his 2000 campaign and hired the *Buffy* creator Joss Whedon to tell him how to sustain credibility by making fun of himself.

Buffy tells the story of a teenage girl in California, the "chosen one" who was born to fight the forces of darkness and save the world. Buffy's town hosts a lot of vampires and various extracurricular demons to keep her busy. Her high school was built on top of a vortex of evil, the Hellmouth. And whose wasn't? The executive producer Joss Whedon once told an interviewer that he was intrigued by "the idea of telling horror stories about high school, since high school was pretty much one long horror story in my life."

High school is the most appropriate metaphor for the 2000 presidential campaign, since high school is the most appropriate metaphor for life in a democratic republic. Because democracy is an idealistic attempt to make life fair. And while high school is the place where you read about the democratic ideal of fairness, it is also the place most of us learn how unfair life really is. Who you are now is informed by who you were then. And every nerd has an anecdote or two to tell about how Nerds versus Jocks is not just some epic mythological struggle but a pesky if normal way of life.

To clarify, playing sports or being a sports fan does not necessarily make person a jock per se. Great athletes are no different from great artists. To me, Reggie Miller shooting a perfect free throw is as beautiful to look at as the bust of Nefertiti in Berlin's Egyptian Museum; watching John McEnroe stirred up the same feelings as listening to the Ramones, and the sportscaster Howard Cosell had one of the great American voices, along with Humphrey Bogart and Snoop Dogg. Also, there's a certain kind of statistically minded sports fan that's an actual subspecies of nerd. Not that they will admit it, as best lampooned in the *Onion* headline "Walking Sports Database Scorns Walking Sci-Fi Database." When I talk about jocks, I'm talking about the sorts of sports enthusiasts that the writer and hockey fan Dave Bidini once described as "dull-witted, chick-baiting dickheads."

When you use the word *jock* around a nerd, the nerd can put a face on it. For my twin sister, the face belongs to the football player who punched her in the jaw in tenth grade. For me, it's a certain gym coach who, during the gym class in the swimming pool, noticed that I just kept walking to the back of the diving board line instead of jumping in the pool. I can't swim. Rather than talking to me about it or spending ten minutes teaching me to swim, the coach blew his whistle and stopped the class. Seventy or so other kids watched him scream me out onto the diving board. He yelled—this is such a gross thing for a grown man to bark at a young girl—*"Kneel down! Kneel down! Kneel down!"* Trying to decide whether I was more afraid of him or of drowning was a real brainteaser. Finally, I just crumpled to my knees and rolled off into the water, flailing my arms until I made it to the side of the pool, gasping. (Two years later, I had the coach as a typing teacher. He taught typing like it was gym for fingers, yelping the command to hit the space bar as though our thumbs were doing push-ups. I like to think of it as real-life *Revenge of the*

Nerds when he assigned the class to type a story and read it aloud and I typed up the swimming pool story and read it to my classmates.) The coach was your basic, cartoonish P.E. teacher fascist. And, as we all know, every democratic republic needs the fascists skulking in dark rooms—be they locker rooms or boardrooms—plotting to humiliate the good people. Even though we will crush their sticks and stones with the punishing blows of our avenging Microsoft Word 6.0.

Buffy the Vampire Slayer is uniquely useful for nerd studies in general and the Gore problem in particular because it includes two nerd characters. Testing any hypothesis requires a control group. Here, the "before" nerd is Giles, Buffy's "watcher"—her protector, teacher, and guide in the ways of demon fighting. He's the school librarian and very, very British. When we meet Willow, Buffy's best friend, she's an A student, a tutor, and a computer whiz. During the show's high school years, the library was the center of Buffy and friends' social universe. Vampire slaying requires an astonishing amount of research. And since Buffy is more of a kick-boxing Valley Girl, Willow handles the necessary Web searches while Giles always has his nose in a moldy old demonology book. Willow is nerd future; Giles is the ghost of nerd past.

Giles is often the butt of Buffy's nerd jokes. When she accuses him of being no fun, he replies,

> "I'll have you know that I have very many relaxing hobbies."
> "Such as?"
> "Well, I enjoy cross-referencing."

111

She might as well have been taunting Al Gore. Once, Giles was talking to Buffy's mother and bemoaning the girl's lack of interest in history. "She lives very much in the now," he says, "and, well, history, of course, is very much about the then."

Doug the *Buffy* writer, talking about Giles, says, "He'll be disdainful of these young Americans for not knowing this stuff. They should know this stuff, Buffy in particular. It's her job, and it will save her life to know this, and she doesn't half the time. She just doesn't do the studying."

In the show's third season, a new Englishman named Wesley showed up. Wesley was even more uptight, even more English than Giles. I was talking to Doug about how the humor regarding the two Englishmen tends to revolve around the way they make no apology for knowing things. I asked him if it was intentional that the two fonts of adult knowledge were British.

"Yeah," Doug says. "Originally, I wanted to make Wesley American. I wanted to base him on George Stephanopoulos. I wanted this obnoxious American know-it-all. And Joss [Whedon—Doug's boss] said, 'No, he has to be British.' You could have gotten some laughs out of an obnoxious, go-go American watcher. But it is off. It doesn't work. The Brits don't apologize for being knowledgeable. In fact, they're a little disdainful of you for not doing your homework. And in America, doing your homework is the most uncool thing in the world."

American democracy is tough. When one of a culture's guiding credos is that "all men are created equal," any person who, say, becomes an expert on, say, nuclear weapons or, say, ecology, i.e., anyone who distinguishes himself through mental excellence, is a nuisance. And anyone, especially a presidential candidate for crying out loud, who doesn't accept this and start falling all over himself to beat everyone else to the punch line, can just go ahead and move to England. In England, even the archconservatives get to be obvious nerds; the Conservative Party's 2001 candidate for prime minister was William Hague, whom *Slate*'s Michael Kinsley has described as a "right-wing dork." "Nevertheless," Kinsley wrote,

> It speaks well of British politics—and the British electorate—that an odd duck like Hague should be leading the ticket of a major political party. It shows that the British still have a long way to go if they aspire to the shallowness and professionalization of American politics. It also shows a cultural tolerance for human diversity that is in some ways more valuable than the legally imposed racial consciousness that goes by the term *diversity* in this country.

In the presidential campaign, the way Gore tried to feign shallow and professional normalcy was by denying his innate nerdiness. Remember all the "alpha male" shenanigans, in which Gore hired a feminist who told him voters would think he was less of a wimp if he wore cowboy boots and khakis? If there's one thing non-nerds hate more than a nerd, it's a nerd pretending to be more virile than he is. Kevin thinks that Gore "should have just made a virtue out of being square. I remember thinking that about Dukakis, who came off very well in Massachusetts when he was just the nerdy guy who got things

113

done. The minute he decided to get in the tank with the Snoopy headgear, he was done."

So how could Gore have become more likable and yet remained true to his wonky self? By taking a few cues from the Willow character on *Buffy*. Willow is not a self-hating nerd. She is a self-deprecating nerd. While Gore, like Giles, is the butt of other people's dork jokes, Willow, a postmodern nerd, peppers her cerebral monologues with one-liners that make light of her own book learning. For instance, substitute-teaching a computer science class she said, "For next time read the chapter on information grouping and binary coding. I bet you'll think coding is pretty cool. If you find two-digit multi-stacked conversions and primary number clusters a big hoot." See what she did there? She neither hid her knowledge nor annoyed anyone. She made knowing arcane specifics seem funny and fun.

When I was talking to Doug the *Buffy* writer about how Gore had missed out on the usefulness of the postmodern nerd's self-deprecating impulse, I couldn't put my finger on what to call it. But at the end of the conversation, I mentioned that I had just finished watching all the *Revenge of the Nerds* movies on videotape. (If you want to up the nerd ante, watch those films and take notes.)

Revenge of the Nerds II is the one where the nerd fraternity attends a frat convention in Florida and all the jock frats want to get rid of the nerds. The jocks dress up as Seminole Indians to try to scare the nerds away. One of the nerds, Poindexter, shouts some gibberish at the "Indians," but nothing happens. He turns to his nerd friend and says, "I don't think those guys are Indians. When I said 'bite my crank' in Seminole, no one responded."

I told Doug, "I was sitting there taking notes and actually yelled at my television, 'Hey, there's no such language as Seminole! The Seminole speak two dialects—Creek and Miccosukee!'"

Doug reflects on this admission for a moment, then asks, "Did you notice that when you told me that story, you did a voice? See? You even did it to yourself. You used the nerd voice!"

The nerd voice. That's what it should be called, that self-deprecating impulse that Gore lacks. Doug's right. I apologized for being a nerd, even when talking privately to another nerd. It was organic, unconscious, I didn't know I was doing it. According to Doug, that's how he and the other *Buffy* writers fashion Willow's nerd voice dialogue. He says there's not "a lot of conscious thought behind it, like, 'Let's put in a disclaimer here.' I think that's just the way we talk. I think everyone on the staff is a recovering nerd. When you declare your genuine passion for something, you are so setting yourself up. You just automatically take the shot before anyone else does. It's this preemptive mockery."

While the preemptive mockery software is automatically included in most nerd brains under the age of forty, it still needs to be installed in Gore. Self-deprecation is not standard baby boomer operating procedure—they were the most aggressive self-aggrandizing generation of the twentieth century and aren't particularly good at making fun of themselves.

Any politician tricky enough to get elected to the House,

not to mention the vice presidency, must necessarily have the kind of postmodern mind which thinks simultaneously about both what he is saying and the way he is saying it. As a national Democrat, Gore has had to frame his arguments about, say, energy policy, remembering that his support base includes both the United Auto Workers and members of the Sierra Club. So he already has the cerebral capability required to give a proper name-heavy speech about the China conundrum followed by an icebreaking wisecrack about not going to the prom. It's silly, demeaning, and time-consuming, for sure, but for a nerd, what part of driving a tank or pulling on cowboy boots is not?

Any person who wants any job, who knows he would be good at the job, knows he has to fake his way through the dumb job interview before he's actually allowed to roll up his sleeves. I asked Doug what he thought would have happened in the campaign if, instead of donning khakis and cowboy boots and French-kissing his wife on TV, Gore had been truer to himself and said what he thought and knew and believed using the nerd voice. Doug didn't hesitate: "Oh my God, he'd be president for life."

I wish it were different. I wish that we privileged knowledge in politicians, that the ones who know things didn't have to hide it behind brown pants, and that the know-not-enoughs were laughed all the way to the Maine border on their first New Hampshire meet and greet. I wish that in order to secure his party's nomination, a presidential candidate would be required to point at the sky and name all the stars; have the periodic table of the elements memorized; rattle off the kings and queens of Spain; define the significance of the Gatling gun; joke around in Latin; interpret the symbolism in seventeenth-century Dutch painting; explain photosynthesis to a six-year-old; recite Emily Dickinson; bake a perfect popover; build a shortwave radio out of a coconut; and know all the words to Hoagy Carmichael's "Two Sleepy People," Johnny Cash's "Five Feet High and Rising," and "You Got the Silver" by the Rolling Stones. After all, the United States is the greatest country on earth dealing with the most complicated problems in the history of the world—poverty, pollution, justice, Jerusalem. What we need is a president who is at least twelve kinds of nerd, a nerd messiah to come along every four years, acquire the Secret Service code name Poindexter, install a *Revenge of the Nerds* screen saver on the Oval Office computer, and one by one decrypt our woes.

Rosa Parks, *C'est Moi*

According to Reuters, on January 20, 2001 in Washington, the special guest at the Florida state inaugural ball was introduced by the country singer Larry Gatlin. He said, "In France it was Joan of Arc; in the Crimea it was Florence Nightingale; in the Deep South there was Rosa Parks; in India there was Mother Teresa, and in Florida there was Katherine Harris."

I leave it to my Indian, Crimean, and French colleagues to determine how the Florida secretary of state is or is not similar to Teresa, Florence, or St. Joan. As for Rosa Parks, Katherine Harris can get in line. Because people around here can't stop comparing themselves to Parks. To wit:

The mayor of Friendship Heights, Maryland, has proposed an outdoor smoking ban because, according to *The Washington Post,* citizens "with asthma or other illnesses 'cannot have full access' to areas where smokers are doing their evil deed. The mayor compares this horrific possibility to Rosa Parks being sent to the back of the bus."

A California dairy farmer protesting the government's milk pricing system poured milk down a drain in front of TV cameras, claiming that he had to take a stand, "just like Rosa Parks had to take a stand."

A street performer in St. Augustine, Florida, is challenging a city ordinance that bans him from doing his act on the town's historic St. George Street. The performer's lawyer told *The Florida Times-Union*, "Telling these people they can exercise their First Amendment rights somewhere other than on St. George is like telling Rosa Parks that she has to sit in the back of the bus." (Which is, coincidentally, also the argument of another Florida lawyer, this one representing adult dancers contesting Tampa's ordinance outlawing lap dancing.) I would also like to mention the rocker, marksman, and conservative activist Ted Nugent, who in his autobiography, *God, Guns and Rock 'n' Roll*, refers to himself as "Rosa Parks with a loud guitar." That's so inaccurate. Everyone knows he's more like Mary Matalin with a fancy deer rifle.

Call me picky, but breathing secondhand smoke, being subject to unfair dairy pricing, and not being able to mime (or lap dance), though they are all tragic, tragic injustices, are not quite as bad as the systematic segregation of *public* transportation based on skin color. And while fighting for your right to lap dance and mime and breathe just the regular pollution is a very fine, very American idea, it is not quite as brave as be-

ing a middle-aged black woman in Alabama in 1955 telling a white man she's not giving him her seat despite the fact that the law requires her to do so. And, oh, by the way, in the process, she gets arrested, and then sparks the Montgomery bus boycott, which is the seed of the civil rights movement as we know it. The bus boycotters not only introduced a twenty-six-year-old pastor by the name of Martin Luther King, Jr., into national public life but, after many months of car pools, walking, and court fights against bus segregation, got the separate but equal doctrine declared illegal once and for all.

It's not just people on the right like Katherine Harris and Ted Nugent who seem especially silly being likened to Parks. I first cringed at this analogy trend at the lefty Ralph Nader's October 2000 campaign rally in Madison Square Garden. Ever sit in a coliseum full of people who think they're heroes? I was surrounded by thousands of well-meaning, well-fed white kids who loved it when the filmmaker Michael Moore told them they should, like Rosa Parks, stand up to power, by which I think he meant vote for Nader so he could qualify for federal matching funds. When Nader himself mentioned abolitionists in Mississippi in 1836 and asked the crowd to "think how lonely it must have been," he was answered, according to my notes, with a "huge, weird cheer." I think I'm a fine enough person—why, the very next morning I was having people over for waffles. But I hope I'm not being falsely modest by pointing out that I'm no Harriet Tubman. And I'm certainly no Rosa Parks. As far as I'm concerned, about the only person in recent memory who has an unimpeachable right to compare himself to Parks is that Chinese student who stared down those tanks in Tiananmen Square.

I was reminded of those Naderites watching a rerun of the sitcom *Sports Night* on Comedy Central. Dan, a television sportscaster played by Josh Charles, has been ordered by his network to make an on-air apology to viewers because he said in a magazine interview that he supports the legalization of marijuana. He stands by his opinion and balks at apologizing. His boss, Isaac (Robert Guillaume), agrees but tells him to do it anyway "because it's television and this is how it's done." Dan replies, "Yeah, well, sitting in the back of the bus was how it was done until a forty-two-year-old lady moved up front." A few minutes later Isaac looks Dan in the eye and tells him, "Because I love you I can say this. No rich young white guy has ever gotten anywhere with me comparing himself to Rosa Parks." Finally, the voice of reason, which of course was heard on a canceled network TV series on cable.

Analogies give order to the world—and solidarity. Pointing out how one person is like another is reassuring, less lonely. Maybe those who would compare their personal inconveniences to the epic struggles of history are just looking for company, and who wouldn't want to be in the company of Rosa Parks? On the other hand, perhaps people who compare themselves to Rosa Parks are simply arrogant, pampered nincompoops with delusions of grandeur who couldn't tell the difference between a paper cut and a decapitation.

In defense of Ted Nugent, the street performer, the mayor, the dairy farmer, the lap dancers, the Naderites, and a fictional sportscaster, I will point out that Katherine Harris is the only person on my list of people lamely compared to a civil rights icon who, at the very moment she was being compared to a civil rights icon, was actually being sued for "massive voter disenfranchisement of people of color during the presidential election"—by the NAACP.

Tom Cruise Makes Me Nervous

During the three-plus hours I sat in the dark watching Paul Thomas Anderson's ensemble epic *Magnolia,* I found myself wanting something I'd never wanted before. More Tom Cruise. As a white, middle-class American moviegoer who graduated from high school during the Reagan administration and subscribes to more than one cable film channel, I've seen every film Tom Cruise ever made, some many more than once, without even trying. Like a Tom Petty or a Jim Lehrer, Cruise falls into that category of competent if ubiquitous public figures that have never won my love or hate and therefore never truly caught my eye. Except for his memorably baroque turn as Lestat in *Interview with the Vampire,* which I, like the rest of the country, blame on his curdled blond hair. But somehow, Cruise's work in *Magnolia,* as the male prowess guru Frank T. J. Mackey, so seized my curiosity that I walked straight out of the theater to go rent his 1983 film *Risky Business.*

Tom Cruise is a mystery in plain sight. If one sets out to explain his appeal, all the normal movie star reasons melt away. For starters, his looks. Cruise has never been a breathtaking beauty. The shock of *Risky Business*, especially if your head's full of the flawless teens currently steaming up the television, is how ordinary Cruise looks. He's a regular, awkward kid, to the extent that I doubt he'd be cast in the lead now. Cruise's face is too angular to be sensual. Whoever said that there are no straight lines in nature never bought a ticket to *The Firm*. His face reminds me more of a math problem than a love poem, the nose and chin right out of high school geometry, hard vectors of flesh. Picasso might have liked to paint him, though it would have been too easy—turning breasts and lips into rectangles is more of a challenge than making a box like Cruise boxier. Even his hair is drawn on with a ruler. Check out his short and sporty coif in *Mission: Impossible*; every individual strand is a line parallel to the y-axis. Which might explain a little of the *Magnolia* draw. Cruise's longer locks in that picture do make his face look a little softer, or as soft as it's possible for a man to look while swaggering around a stage inciting other men to date rape proclaiming, "Respect the cock!"

I'd never given Tom Cruise's cock much thought before. If I had been asked to draw a nude Tom Cruise before seeing the bulge protruding out of his white underwear as he strips in *Magnolia*, I probably would have given him the smooth anatomy of a Ken doll. Where Tom Cruise sticks his privates has been the subject of rumors and lawsuits, but I never gave Cruise's sexuality much truck one way or the other. Because, watching his movies over the past couple of weeks, I am con-

stantly surprised when Cruise is in the same room with another person, much less the same bed. He strikes me as ut-
terly, quintessentially, fundamentally alone. Of course Stanley
Kubrick wanted Cruise to play the doctor in his *Eyes Wide
Shut*. Much of the movie requires the doctor to walk the
streets of New York by himself at night, and when a director
needs alone-in-a-crowd, he calls Tom Cruise. The running gag
about his title character in *Jerry Maguire* was that Jerry hates
to be alone, but he also can't connect with anyone. In that
sense, *Jerry Maguire* is the perfect fable of America's relation-
ship with Tom Cruise. Basically, we think he's a stuck-up
phony and we want to see him hit bottom, have his love interest notice for once that he isn't paying any attention to her,
and then we want to see him humanized, i.e., cry. Cruise's
first two Oscar nominations—for *Jerry Maguire* and *Born on
the Fourth of July*—display the public's deep desire to see him
put through a ringer. We want him to get his legs cut off (*July*),
and we want to see him lose for a while to the even slicker, if
that's possible, Jay Mohr (*Maguire*) because we want to punish
him. Because I think the only reason seemingly every man,
woman, and child in America goes to see his movies is not that
he blinds us with beauty or talent or emotion. We can't take
our eyes off him because he makes us a little nervous. Not
too nervous—that's why we invented Dennis Hopper. Cruise
makes us stealth nervous, just jittery enough to keep us
awake.

Watch Barry Levinson's *Rain Man* again and I guarantee
you that the discomfort of Dustin Hoffman's shticky autism
does not compare to the heebie-jeebies of Cruise's perfor-

mance. Hoffman can dodder on about missing *Jeopardy!* every thirteen seconds and he's fresh air, but Cruise, closed off and angry, is a twitch fest. When Hoffman's Raymond throws a fit as Cruise tries to give him a hug, the viewer more than understands. While autism is the most natural thing in the world, an embrace from Cruise defies the laws of nature. When the cute little kid in *Jerry Maguire* gave Cruise a hug, my first reaction was parental. I wanted to grab the child away, scolding, "We don't do that. We don't touch burning stoves, strangers' candy, and we do not touch Tom Cruise." Because Cruise is not, as the French say, good in his skin. Even in his most flawless, most affable performance, as Lt. Daniel Kaffee in *A Few Good Men,* Cruise seems the most comfortable on the softball field, having conversations with Demi Moore through a fence. Because Tom Cruise is the most talented actor of all time at keeping his distance.

Like most screen icons, Tom Cruise is not of us. Us, with our faces lumped together out of concentric circles versus his straight-edge mug. Us with our nerves and fears and him with his lieutenant-lawyer cockiness. Him with his choreographed cocktails and us dripping gin on our carpets as olives splash on the floor. But that's where Tom Cruise stops—better than. There's no further inspiration to be gained. Like every time I see *To Kill a Mockingbird* I take one look at Gregory Peck's Atticus Finch and resolve to become more dignified. Even seeing Rene Russo in the remake of *The Thomas Crown Affair* made me vow to dress better, which, if not a moral for our times, is at least some little something. Cruise's best line in *Magnolia* comes when his character is asked by the reporter interview-

THE PARTLY CLOUDY PATRIOT

ing him why he's stopped talking. "I'm quietly judging you," he seethes, and that might be just what we're afraid of with regards to Tom Cruise.

The mark of a great performance is that it obliterates distance, gets under our skin. It's simply harder for an icon to do that. But possible. *Magnolia* is the first time Cruise even comes close. It is far and away his most physical performance. If only because I'd never heard him breathe. About half of Cruise's on-screen time is taken up with Mackey's rooster struts—again, alone—across a darkened stage. His entrance, a ridiculous backlit pose to the strains of "Also Sprach Zarathustra," isn't his only Elvis move. His debauched bumps and grinds as he speaks, often fucking the air, punctuate his hilarious pigspeak with a new earthiness. He'd never seemed more human—which is to say funnier, more vulnerable—than playing a man without the self-awareness to know that barking the words "you are gonna give me that cherry pie sweet mama baby" might make him come off dopey, pathetic, and sad. We've never seen Cruise this lewd, and thus we've never really seen him get his hands dirty, dirty with the dopiness of desire. As my upstanding mother said when she called last night to tell me why she'd walked out of "that horrible, horrible *Magnolia*" and wanted me to explain what's wrong with movies today, she sighed, "I'll never be able to look at Tom Cruise again." I didn't have the heart to tell her that I feel like I've seen him for the first time.

Underground Lunchroom

I am a rube who reads guidebooks. That is how I learned that the Old Faithful Inn at Yellowstone National Park is the world's largest log structure, and that one may sit on its balcony and sip a gin and tonic while watching Old Faithful spout off. Another guidebook tipped me off that visitors to Theodore Roosevelt National Park in North Dakota may partake in the nearby town's "Pitchfork Fondue," in which rib eye steaks are speared on the ends of pitchforks and dunked in barrels of boiling oil—crispy, theatrical meat as the sun goes down over the Badlands.

In this fondness for these things, I am not alone. For I have sat on picnic tables among my countrymen, some of whom stood down the Nazis, and we've smiled at the landscape and at one another, the grease trickling onto our souvenir T-shirts.

As I was paging through a guidebook entry on New Mexico's Carlsbad Caverns National Park, the words "Underground Lunchroom" caught my eye. The lunchroom is smack-dab in the middle of the caverns, 750 feet underground. The guidebook warned, "To modern eyes, this strange installation seems absurd, but moves to close it down have been stymied by its place in popular affections." As I would come to find out, it is a restaurant so oddly placed that it requires an act of Congress repeated every year to keep going.

If the geological marvels of Carlsbad Caverns came into being in the time before history, the Underground Lunchroom represents the time before arugula. Established in 1926, the lunchroom was renovated in the 1970s, and it shows. The food and souvenir stations are housed in sandy brown booths that remind me of the drive-through bank architecture of my childhood. The food—box lunches of cold chicken or ham sandwiches, wedges of pie in plastic, wedge-shaped containers—is the sort of fare my grade school washed down with Shasta cola on the Freedom Train field trip in '76. Not long after the Bicentennial, middle Americans started eating better and dressing better and calling nature "the environment," but the Underground Lunchroom is a throwback to our unpretentious if unenlightened past.

The National Park Service wanted to get rid of it. In 1991 they began an environmental assessment of the lunchroom. Money was spent. Scientists conferred. It took two years. And, sadly for them, they were unable to find any evidence that food particles, Freon gas in the refrigerators, or the use of microwave ovens was harming the ecosystem and climate of the cave. In fact, all sorts of things pose a bigger ecological threat to the cave than the lunchroom does, like the existence of lights, of an elevator, of actual, bacteria-carrying tourists with their lint-covered clothing.

In the end, the reason the Park Service wants to close the lunchroom is not thanks to science. It has to do with aesthetics. In the years since the lunchroom was built, we as a people have gone through a grand tectonic shift in the way we think about national parks. Basically, we don't believe in putting crap in the middle of nature anymore. And not only that, we believe in taking out as much of the old crap as possible. This was codified in a 1991 Park Service policy called the Vail Agenda, which clearly states, "The National Park Service should use existing authority to remove, wherever possible, unnecessary facilities."

It's the aesthetics of all this that Ed Greene talks about when we walk through the cavern and he makes the case for the removal of the lunchroom. Greene is in charge of visitor services at Carlsbad Caverns National Park. He contributed to that environmental study. And he spends so much time underground amidst the marvels of the cavern that he has a separate name for the world that you and I inhabit. He calls that world the "surface world."

"It's hard to describe this for someone who can't see it because there's nothing in the surface world experience that prepares people to see something like this," Greene tells me. "It is just unlike anything else on earth. There will be times that I will intentionally, if I'm having a rough day or something is getting under my skin a little bit, I'll just intentionally come down in the cave and find a place just to sit and soak this up. This resource and this kind of beauty keep me humbled and keep me on the right path to do the things that I need to be doing here. Nobody created Carlsbad Caverns so that they could have lunch 750 feet underground. If you walk down through the natural entrance, what you are experiencing is this natural creation, and then as you exit out of that area and you walk into this area there's this stark contrast. That's the first thing you see when you walk out. You are coming to one of the world's great natural attractions, one of the greatest attractions in all creation, and what do you see? Something not unlike maybe a mall somewhere."

If the Park Service reasoning for removing the Underground Lunchroom is essentially an aesthetic argument, the main reason to save the lunchroom is equally aesthetic. Namely, it's cool to eat lunch in a cave. You can also mail a postcard from the lunchroom and stamp it "Mailed 750 Feet Underground." It's entertaining to mail a postcard in a cave. The lunchroom even has a bank of pay phones. Why would you need to make a telephone call from the cave? Well, you wouldn't *need* to. You might do it because it's fun, and you're on vacation, and you're at a place with the word *park* in its name.

The Carlsbad business community partly depends on vacationers for their livelihood. A local Carlsbad company called Cavern Supply has operated the lunchroom since the 1920s and employs around sixty people in the summer. In a town of 25,000 people, this is significant.

Frank Hodnett is the president of Cavern Supply. He runs the lunchroom. His view, which is not entirely self-serving, is shared by many in the Carlsbad community, who believe that

the concessions associated with the cave are part of the cave's history. He worked in the cave as a little boy, standing on top of Coke cases to make change. He was accompanying his father, who was also an employee of Cavern Supply. Hodnett's father started working at the lunchroom in the twenties. Back before the elevators, Hodnett senior carried the food in and out of the cave every day on his back, acquiring the nickname Yo Yo. For Frank Hodnett, his own family history here is intertwined with the thousands of families he's fed at the lunchroom's tables.

"Hundreds and thousands of people have eaten here," Hodnett says, "and every one of them has said that that was one of their memorable things that happened in the cave. You talk to people now that are fifty, sixty years old and they will say, 'I remember when we went through the caverns and we stopped and had one of those sandwiches.' "

So when the National Park Service announced their plans to remove the Underground Lunchroom, the Carlsbad Chamber of Commerce opposed them.

Gary Perkowski is the mayor of Carlsbad. Like a lot of locals, he also worked in the Underground Lunchroom as a teenager. He was one of the people from Carlsbad who argued the lunchroom's merits before one of New Mexico's congressmen, Representative Joe Skeen.

"I think Representative Skeen has always been on our side," Mayor Perkowski asserts. "He works closely with the leaders of Carlsbad on numerous projects, and we just went to Washington, explained our position and what we thought. And he agreed with us."

"That's it?" I wondered.

"That's basically it. He agreed with our position and did everything he could to make sure that was implemented."

I'll say. Consider the following legislation prepared by Representative Skeen's committee. According to H.R. 2217, the Department of Interior and Related Agencies Appropriations Act, 2002, Section 307, "None of the funds made available by this Act may be obligated or expended by the National Park Service to enter into or implement a concession contract which permits or requires the removal of the underground lunchroom at the Carlsbad Caverns National Park." That is the same language that has appeared in every Department of Interior appropriations bill since 1994, and what it means is that the National Park Service is barred from using federal funds to close down the Underground Lunchroom. (Calls to Representative Skeen's office for comment were not returned.)

The National Park Service is obeying the will of Congress, but you don't get the feeling they're all that happy about it. If the Park Service were a person, the Underground Lunchroom would be one of the dumb mistakes it made as a kid. It's like Congress is telling it that not only can it not remove the tattoo it got one drunken night in the twenties but it has to invite 300,000 people a year to look at it. And that's how a lot of employees think about it too, as a youthful gaffe.

Cave specialist Ron Kerbo, who was one of the authors of the study calling for the lunchroom's abolition, remembers going there when he was little: "Like any eight-year-old, I thought it was pretty interesting to be able to eat in the cave. And I particularly remember the pickles. They used to have these shelves with these small paper cups with pickles in them and you could eat as many of those as you wanted. So I was always fond of eating the pickles in the Underground Lunchroom."

Still, he says, there's no reason for the lunchroom today. Food is available to tourists in a restaurant that's just fifty-seven seconds away by elevator. And for all the visitors who enter the cavern through the elevator, the lunchroom is the first and last thing they see.

"In that environment," Kerbo says, "it seems to me, eating in the lunchroom mars the visitor's experience in the cave."

"When you were eight years old, did you feel marred?" I ask him.

"While, yes, as a child, I ate in there and I enjoyed it and I did remember it. But I have moved on. And the great thing that the national parks teach us is that if we are attuned to these natural processes, then we can move on. If your only memory of Carlsbad Caverns is eating in the lunchroom, then you have missed the essence of the experience."

Everything he says is true. But I found his reasoning frustrating because my only available counterargument is that the Underground Lunchroom is a lark. And what's the dignity in that? I'm jealous of Kerbo's certainty, which is both idealistic and logical. My small life in the surface world is a contradictory, hypocritical mess in which I scowl through newspaper articles about the abuses of the timber industry while sitting in my maple chair next to my maple bookcase. Isn't that how most of us live in this country?

I spent a couple of hours walking down through the caverns, and this is what I saw. I saw fourteen football fields of treasures—things with names like Witch's Finger, Totem Pole, and Mirror Lake, formations described as popcorn and soda straws in places called the Boneyard, the Hall of Giants, the Big Room. How very human to measure nature in sports arenas, describe it as snack food, map its contours as if we're drawing rectangles on the blueprint of an office building. I can't do any better. I don't know how to describe the magnificence of Carlsbad Caverns without making it sound like a cartoon or a drug trip or a cartoon of a drug trip. The only thing I can say is that it is one of those dear places that make you love the world.

So when I came to the end of the last trail, I wasn't quite ready to say good-bye to the cave. I felt all dreamy, and I didn't want the feeling to end. If only there were some way station, some transitional zone between this world and the surface world above, a place to sit and ponder my own insignificance.

I sleepwalk to a picnic table in the Underground Lunchroom. When I first read about the lunchroom in the guidebook, I'd never suspected it could feel so contemplative. Then I rip open a bag of barbecue potato chips and listen to the sound of my own teeth crunching. I am capable of chewing and pondering at the same time.

Since the lunchroom does no significant harm to the caverns' ecology, I'd like to believe that this is one of those lucky places where we don't have to choose between doing the right thing and enjoying a goof. I look up at the ceiling of the lunchroom, which is, of course, the ceiling of the cave. It looks so lunar I can't help but think of a certain astronaut. In 1971, *Apollo*

14's Alan Shepard hit golf balls on the moon. Gearing up to face the profundity of the universe, this man brought sporting goods with him into space. Who can blame him? That's what we Americans do when we find a place that's really special. We go there and act exactly like ourselves. And we are a bunch of fun-loving dopes.

Wonder Twins

In December 1999, the Associated Press released a photograph of Luther and Johnny Htoo, twelve-year-old twin brothers commanding a ragtag guerrilla army in the rain forest of Myanmar (formerly Burma). In the picture, the little boys are side by side. Johnny's the serene one with the angel eyes. Luther, forehead shaved, is the smirking devil sucking down a cigar. For several weeks, I couldn't open a magazine without seeing that photo of the twins, without reading of their bizarre cult of soldiers called God's Army, of their attack on a Thai hospital in which they held some five hundred people hostage. Every time I saw the picture the first thing that popped into my head was this: I miss my sister.

I am a twin. And to be a twin child is to always have another person in the picture. My mother made a halfhearted stab at keeping separate photo albums for each of us. But the distinctions are arbitrary. Amy is in most of the faded black-and-white snapshots in mine, and vice versa.

Once I saw Luther and Johnny sharing the same frame, it hit me how much they have in common with my sister and me. The similarities are uncanny. Luther and Johnny were illiterate, Baptist, messianic insurgents struggling against the government of Myanmar, and my sister Amy and I shared a locker all through junior high.

Some of my friends couldn't stop talking about the Htoo twins. They would speak of them in a single breath—LutherandJohnny. "Did you see the photo of LutherandJohnny?" or "I'm obsessed with LutherandJohnny." And I pine for that, that single name, especially now that my sister and I live so far apart. I miss the way I was never Sarah and my sister was never Amy, but we were together AmyandSarah. Unlike the identicals, who act as photocopies of each other, we're fraternal. Which means that we're not doubles so much as halves. We're split down the middle. I'm a single careerist with a walk-up apartment in New York City; she's a married, dog-owning mother in Montana with a, swear to God, white picket fence. People love that about us, love that I can't sew on a button but she makes quilts. That's why people respond to the Luther and Johnny picture. They adore the contrast between the pretty, girlish Johnny and the hyena-faced Luther. Meet Joan of Arc and her brother Genghis Khan.

Will Luther and Johnny's memories meld? Up until around the age of ten, my sister and I often cannot remember who was doing what and who was watching, who got thrown from what horse, who got spanked for what trespass, who committed the trespass that led to the spanking. (Well, it was usually Amy, so ill-behaved. When I called her to talk about Luther and Johnny, she had seen the photo and knew what I was thinking. "I'm Luther!" she screamed into the phone.) So years from now, when Luther and Johnny look back on the exciting terrorist period of their lives, will Johnny ask Luther, "Was it you who threw that hand grenade on the government sniper or was it me?" Maybe Luther will say to Johnny, "Help me out here, but I can't remember which one of us shot the papaya off that dumb orphan's head."

In January 2001, the Htoo twins turned themselves in to Thai border guards, admitted they had no magical powers, and asked for their mommy. But while they still lived out there in the killing fields, Luther and Johnny had it easy twin-wise. In the bush, they didn't have to deal with the aftermath of those periodic cable TV documentaries on twins. They've probably never been cornered at some dinner party with an HBO subscriber who quizzes them on "like the weirdest show I've ever seen about these freaks, I mean twins, who were separated at birth and everything and still held their cigarettes at the same angle even though they didn't meet until adulthood and I was just wondering if when your sister feels pain you feel it too?" So Luther or Johnny will never have to hover over the lukewarm hummus and inform some only child that just because you're a twin it doesn't mean you're some kind of life-size voodoo doll and that if you have some kind of psychic powers at all they have nothing to do with your twin but rather with peculiar celebrities, like when you dreamed you said hi to Kevin Spacey on the street and the next morning he received an Oscar nomination or the fact that you happened to be talking about the Dallas Cowboys coach Tom Landry the night he died.

(Another dignified plus of being a twin without television is that Luther and Johnny have probably never watched the cartoon *Superfriends,* the one in which Aquaman and Superman and Wonder Woman teamed up to fight global crime. And thus, Luther and Johnny, unlike my sister and me, will never have to cringe at the memory of imitating the goody-goody, tights-wearing minor characters known as the Wonder Twins. Thus they'll escape the embarrassment of having said the words "Wonder Twin powers, activate! Form of . . . a straight-A student.")

The advantage of being a twelve-year-old guerrilla warrior in terms of twin self-esteem is not unlike the advantage of attending a private school—the uniforms. As American public school graduates, my sister and I know the trappings, the symbolism, of clothes. When we were toddlers, our mother dressed us alike. And if we weren't wearing the same dress, we wore the same style in different colors. If she wore baby blue, I wore pink. If she wore navy blue, I wore red. Until the moment when we were maybe five and Amy informed our mother, "Mama, I don't want my dress to be like Sarah's." In high school, she wore blue, I wore black. She wore pink and I wore black. Luther and Johnny, in their makeshift camo, will never go through that, the stereotyping, never know what it's like to be labeled the gloomy, plain Jane or the girlie-girl blonde. Then again, they won't crack themselves up by being the gloomy plain Jane and buying a red satin dress in front of

THE PARTLY CLOUDY PATRIOT

Mom, just to see the look on her face. On the other hand, Amy and Sarah will never know the satisfaction of a job well done that comes with leading an army of children to their death.

Someday, when Luther and Johnny are older—perhaps in exile—they'll flip through their photo albums as my sister and I do at Christmas. Will they look fondly on the smoker-non-smoker snapshot the way we giggle over the Polaroid from 1974 in which Amy has thrown up on me in bed but I slept right through it and she thought it so hilarious she woke up my parents to get the camera and there she is, in color with the light on, smiling and pointing as I lie there peacefully, my Snoopy pajamas soaked in puke? Or the Sears portrait when we're not yet two and I am blank and placid on the shag carpet fondling a plastic football and Amy's a fidgeting glare, the light bouncing off her hot tears? Or perhaps Luther and Johnny, who reportedly cannot read, have never seen the photo and never will and so they'll be less inclined to typecast each other the way everyone else does, the way I was the dark one and she was the blue-eyed blonde, the way I was the "smart" one and she was the "fun" one even though she's really sharp and I'd like to think I'm not a total drag. Maybe, unlike someone who shall remain Amy, Luther is too caught up with training his blindfolded child followers in disassembling rifles to taunt Johnny with the fact that he was almost eight and still had training wheels on his banana-seat pink bike even though he, Luther, had been riding in the driveway solo since he was four.

At twelve, Luther and Johnny probably already suspected twindom's secret lesson. Namely, that no matter what they accomplished—who they trained, inspired, or killed—their greatest allure might be the circumstances of their birth. That to be a twin and to distinguish oneself besides is a bit of overkill. My sister and I were about their age when our family moved north. At our new school, we lived the preteen girl's nightmare: we stuck out. We were not just new kids, and we were not just new kids with funny Okie accents. We were new kids with funny Okie accents and twins besides. It was more than our classmates could bear. The famous photo of Luther and Johnny catches them on the cusp of this twinly dread—of being too famous for too much too fast.

Cowboys v. Mounties

Canada haunts me. The United States's neighbor to the north first caught my fancy a few years back when I started listening to the CBC. I came for the long-form radio documentaries; I stayed for the dispatches from the Maritimes and Guelph. On the CBC, all these nice people, seemingly normal but for the hockey obsession, had a likable knack for loving their country in public without resorting to swagger or hate.

A person keen on all things French is called a Francophile. One who has a thing for England is called an Anglophile. An admirer of Germany in the 1930s and '40s is called Pat Buchanan. But no word has been coined to describe Americans obsessed with Canada, not that dictionary publishers have been swamped with requests. The comedian Jon Stewart used to do a bit in which a Canadian woman asked him to come clean with what Americans *really* think of Canada. "We don't," he said.

Keeping track of Canadians is like watching a horror movie. It's *Invasion of the Body Snatchers* in slow-mo. They look like us, but there's something slightly, eerily off. Why is that? The question has nagged me for years. Asking why they are the way they are begs the follow-up query about how we ended up this way too.

There's a sad sack quality to the Canadian chronology I find entirely endearing. I once asked the CBC radio host Ian Brown how on earth one could teach Canadian schoolchildren their history in a way that could be remotely inspiring, and he answered, "It isn't inspiring."

Achieving its independence from Britain gradually and cordially, through polite meetings taking place in nice rooms, Canada took a path to sovereignty that is one of the most hilariously boring stories in the world. One Canadian history textbook I have describes it thus, "British North Americans moved through the 1850s and early sixties towards a modestly spectacular resolution of their various ambitions and problems." Modestly spectacular. Isn't that adorable?

One day, while nonchalantly perusing the annals of Canadian history, I came across mention of the founding of the Mounties. The Royal Canadian Mounted Police, called the North-West Mounted Police at its inception, was created, I read, to establish law and order on the Canadian frontier in anticipation of settlement and the Canadian Pacific Railroad. In 1873, Canada's first prime minister, John Macdonald, saw what was happening in the American Wild West and organized a police force to make sure Canada steered clear of America's bloodbath.

That's it. Or, as they might say in Quebec, voilà! That explains how the Canadians are different from Americans. No cowboys for Canada. Canada got Mounties instead—Dudley Do-Right, not John Wayne. It's a mind-set of "Here I come to save the day" versus "Yippee-ki-yay, motherfucker." Or maybe it's chicken and egg: The very idea that the Canadian head of state would come to the conclusion that establishing law and order *before* large numbers of people migrated west, to have rules and procedures and authorities waiting for them, is anathema to the American way.

Not only did the Mounties aim to avoid the problems we had faced on our western frontier, especially the violent, costly Indian wars, they had to clean up after our spillover mess. In a nineteenth-century version of that drug-war movie *Traffic*, evil American whiskey traders were gouging and poisoning Canadian Indian populations. Based in Fort Benton, Montana, they sneaked across the border to peddle their rotgut liquor, establishing illegal trading posts, including the infamous Fort Whoop-up, in what is now Alberta. You can't throw a dart at a map of the American West without hitting some mass grave or battleground—Sand Creek, Little Bighorn, Wounded Knee— but it's fitting that the most famous such Canadian travesty, the Cypress Hills Massacre, happened because American whiskey and fur traders were exacting revenge on a few Indians believed to have stolen their horses. The Americans slaughtered between one and two hundred Assiniboine men, women, and children. Never mind that the horse thieves had been Cree. That was 1873. The Mounties were under formation, but they hadn't yet marched west.

The most remarkable thing about the Mounties was their mandate: one law. One law for everyone, Indian or white. The United States makes a big to-do about all men being created equal, but we're still working out the kinks of turning that idea into actual policy. Reporting to the force's commissioner in 1877, one Mountie wrote of Americans in his jurisdiction, "These men always look upon the Indians as their natural enemies, and it is their rule to shoot at them if they approach after being warned off. I was actually asked the other day by an American who has settled here, if we had the same law here as on the other side, and if he was justified in shooting any Indian who approached his camp after being warned not to in advance."

Word of the Canadians' fairness got around. Some northwestern tribes referred to the border between the United States and Canada as the "medicine line." Robert Higheagle, a Lakota Sioux from Sitting Bull's band, recalled, "They told us this line was considered holy. They called that a holy trail. They believe things are different when you cross from one side to another. You are altogether different. On one side you are perfectly free to do as you please. On the other you are in danger."

To Canada's dismay, the northern side of the medicine line became an attractive destination for American Indians, including the most famous, most difficult one of all, Sitting Bull. On the run after Little Bighorn, Sitting Bull and entourage settled near Canada's Fort Walsh, under the command of Major James Walsh. Walsh and, as he called him, Bull became such great friends that the Canadian government had Walsh transferred to another post to separate him from Sitting Bull. Sitting Bull was an American problem and the Canadian government wanted to boot him south. Walsh even defied orders and went to Chicago to lobby on Sitting Bull's behalf, but to no avail, ensuring that Sitting Bull would die south of the medicine line.

All the Sitting Bull complications make Walsh my favorite Mountie. But he's a very American choice—he bucked the system, he played favorites for a friend, he defied policy, he stuck out. (Apparently, even having a favorite Mountie is an American trait. When I asked the twentieth commissioner of Mounties, Giuliano "Zach" Zaccardelli, who was his favorite RCMP commissioner in history, he answered Canadianly, "Every one of them has contributed tremendously to the legacy of the RCMP, and I hope that during my tenure I will be able to add some value to the legacy that those nineteen who came before me left for this organization.") When Walsh heard that Sitting Bull had been fatally shot in Minnesota, he wrote, "Bull's ambition is I am afraid too great to let him settle down and be content with an uninteresting life." This strikes me as almost treasonously individualistic, with American shades of "pursuit of happiness" and "liberty or death."

Everyone knows what the individualistic American cowboy fetish gets us: shot. It all comes down to guns. The population of the United States is ten times that of Canada, but we have about thirty times more firearms. Two-thirds of our homicides are committed with firearms, compared with one-third of theirs. (Which begs the question, just what are Canadian killers using, hair dryers tossed into bathtubs?)

The famous (well, in Canada) historian Pierre Berton, in his surprisingly out-of-print book *Why We Act Like Canadians*, informs an American friend that it has to do with weather. Having been to Edmonton in January, I cede his point. He wrote,

> Hot weather and passion, gunfights and race riots go together. Your mythic encounters seem to have taken place at high noon, the sun beating down on a dusty Arizona street. I find it difficult to contemplate a similar gunfight in Moose Jaw, in the winter, the bitter rivals struggling vainly to shed two pairs of mitts and reach under several layers of parka for weapons so cold that the slightest touch of flesh on steel would take the skin off their thumbs.

Most of the time, I feel Canadian. I live a quiet life. I own no firearms (though, as a gunsmith's daughter, I stand to inherit a freaking arsenal). I revere the Bill of Rights, but at the same time I believe that anyone who's using three or more of them at a time is hogging them too much. I'm a newspaper-reading, French-speaking, radio-documentary-loving square. A lot of my favorite comedians, such as Martin Short, Eugene Levy, the Kids in the Hall, are Canadian. I like that self-deprecating Charlie Brown sense of humor. As Canadian-born *Saturday Night Live* producer Lorne Michaels once put it in a panel discussion devoted to the question of why Canadians are so funny at the Ninety-second Street Y, a Canadian would never have made a film called *It's a Wonderful Life* because "that would be bragging." The Canadian version, he said, would have been titled "It's an All Right Life."

So I mostly walk the Canadian walk, but the thing about a lot of Canadian talk is that it sounds bad. When I went to Ottawa, the "Washington of the North," to see the RCMP's Musical Ride, which is sort of like synchronized swimming on horseback, I was telling a constable in the Mounties about a new U.S. Army recruiting ad. The slogan was "an army of one." It aimed to reassure American kids that they wouldn't be nameless, faceless nobodies, that they could join the army and still do their own thing.

The Mountie was horrified. He said, "I think we have to try and work as a team and work together. If you start to be an individualist, then everybody's going their own way. One person might be doing something and the other person might be doing something else and everybody wants to put their word in and thinks, I'm better than him or My idea's better than his. You need conformity. You need everybody to stick together and work as a team."

It hurt my ears when he said "you need conformity." I know he's probably right, and what organization more than a military one requires lockstep uniformity so that fewer people get killed? But still. No true American would ever talk up the virtue of conformity. Intellectually, I roll my eyes at the cowboy outlaw ethic, but in my heart I know I buy into it a little, that it's a deep part of my identity. Once, when I was living in Holland, I went to the movies, and when a Marlboro Man ad came on the screen, I started bawling with homesickness. I may be the only person who cried all the way through *Don't Tell Mom the Babysitter's Dead.*

The Mounties on the Musical Ride dress in the old-fashioned red serge suits and Stetson hats, like Dudley Do-Right. Seeing them on their black horses, riding in time to music, was entirely lovable, yet lacking any sort of, for lack of a better word, edge. I tried to ask some of them about it.

I say, "In the States, the Mountie is a squeaky-clean icon. Does that ever bother you that the Mountie is not 'cool'?"

He stares back blankly. I ask him, "You know what I mean?"

"No, I don't."

"There's no dark side," I tell him. "The Mounties have no dark side."

He laughs. "That might be one of the things that upset the Americans, because we're just that much better." Then he feels so bad about this little put-down that he repents, backtracking about how "there's good and bad in everybody," that Americans and Canadians "just have different views," and that "Canadians are no better than anyone else."

Another constable, overhearing, says, "Our country is far younger than the United States, but at the same time, the United States is a young country when you compare it to the countries of Europe."

"Yeah," I answer, "but you're a very well-behaved young country."

"Well"—he smiles—"that's just the way my mum raised me."

The Partly Cloudy Patriot

In the summer of 2000, I went to see the Mel Gibson block-buster *The Patriot*. I enjoyed that movie. Watching a story line like that is always a relief. Of course the British must be expelled, just as the Confederates must surrender, Hitler must be crushed, and yee-haw when the Red Sea swallows those slave-mongering Egyptians. There were editorials about *The Patriot*, the kind that always accompany any historical film, written by professors who insist things nobody cares about, like Salieri wasn't that bad a sort or the fact that Roman gladiators maybe didn't have Australian accents. A little anachronism is part of the fun, and I don't mind if in real life General Cornwallis never lost a battle in the South as he does rather gloriously in the film. Isn't art supposed to improve on life?

Personally, I think there was more than enough historical accuracy in *The Patriot* to keep the spoilsports happy. Because I'm part spoilsport on my father's side, and I felt nagged with quandaries every few minutes during the nearly three-hour film. American history is a quagmire, and the more one knows, the quaggier the mire gets. If you're paying attention during *The Patriot* and you know your history and you have a stake in that history, not to mention a conscience, the movie is not an entirely cartoonish march to glory. For example, Mel Gibson's character, Benjamin Martin, is conflicted. He doesn't want to fight the British because he still feels bad about chopping up some Cherokee into little pieces during the French and Indian War. Since I'm a part-Cherokee person myself, Gibson lost a little of the sympathy I'd stored up for him because he'd been underrated in *Conspiracy Theory*. And did I mention his character lives in South Carolina? So by the end of the movie, you look at the youngest Mel junior bundled in his mother's arms and think, Mel just risked his life so that that kid's kids can rape their slaves and vote to be the first state to secede from the Union.

The Patriot did confirm that I owe George Washington an apology. I always liked George fine, though I dismissed him as a mere soldier. I prefer the pen to the sword, so I've always been more of a Jeffersonhead. The words of the Declaration of Independence are so right and true that it seems like its poetry alone would have knocked King George III in the head. Like, he would have read this beloved passage, "We hold these Truths to be self-evident, that all Men are created equal, that they are endowed by their Creator with certain unalienable Rights—that among these are Life, Liberty, and the pursuit of Happiness," and thought the notion so just, and yet still so wonderfully whimsical, that he would have dethroned himself on the spot. But no, it took a grueling, six-year-long war to make independence a fact.

I rarely remember this. In my ninety-five-cent copy of the Declaration of Independence and the Constitution, the two documents are separated by only a blank half page. I forget that there are eleven years between them, eleven years of war and the whole Articles of Confederation debacle. In my head, the two documents are like the A side and B side of the greatest single ever released that was recorded in one great drunken night, but no, there's a lot of bleeding life between them. Dead boys and dead Indians and Valley Forge.

Anyway, *The Patriot*. The best part of seeing it was standing in line for tickets. I remember how jarring it was to hear my fellow moviegoers say that word. "Two for *The Patriot* please." "One for *The Patriot* at 5:30." For years, I called it the *P* word, because it tended to make nice people flinch. For the better part of the 1990s, it seemed like the only Americans who publicly described themselves as patriots were scary militia types hiding out in the backwoods of Michigan and Montana, cleaning their guns. One of the few Americans still celebrating Patriot's Day—a nearly forgotten holiday on April 19 commemorating the Revolutionary War's first shots at Lexington and Concord—did so in 1995 by murdering 168 people in the federal building in Oklahoma City. In fact, the same week I saw *The Patriot*, I was out with some friends for dessert. When I asked a fellow named Andy why he had chosen a cupcake with a little American flag stuck in the frosting, I expected him to say that he was in a patriotic mood, but he didn't. He said that he was "feeling jingoistic."

Well, that was a long time ago. As I write this, it's December
2001 in New York City. The only words one hears more often
than variations on *patriot* are "in the wake of," "in the aftermath of," and "since the events of September 11." We also use
the word *we* more. Patriotism as a word and deed has made a
comeback. At Halloween, costume shops did a brisk business
in Uncle Sam and Betsy Ross getups. Teen pop bombshell
Britney Spears took a breather during her live telecast from
Vegas's MGM Grand to sit on a piano bench with her belly
ring glinting in the spotlight and talk about "how proud I am of
our nation right now." Chinese textile factories are working
overtime to fill the consumer demand for American flags.

Immediately after the attack, seeing the flag all over the
place was moving, endearing. So when the newspaper I sub-
scribe to published a full-page, full-color flag to clip out and
hang in the window, how come I couldn't? It took me a while
to figure out why I guiltily slid the flag into the recycling bin
instead of taping it up. The meaning had changed; or let's say
it changed back. In the first day or two the flags were plastered
everywhere, seeing them was heartening because they indi-
cated that we're all in this sorrow together. The flags were
purely emotional. Once we went to war, once the president
announced that we were going to retaliate against the "evildo-
ers," then the flag again represented what it usually represents, the government. I think that's when the flags started
making me nervous. The true American patriot is by definition
skeptical of the government. Skepticism of the government
was actually one of the platforms the current figurehead of the
government ran on. How many times in the campaign did

President Bush proclaim of his opponent, the then vice president, "He trusts the federal government and I trust the people"? This deep suspicion of Washington is one of the most American emotions an American can have. So by the beginning of October, the ubiquity of the flag came to feel like peer pressure to always stand behind policies one might not necessarily agree with. And, like any normal citizen, I prefer to make up my mind about the issues of the day on a case by case basis at 3:00 A.M. when I wake up from my *Nightline*-inspired nightmares.

One Independence Day, when I was in college, I was living in a house with other students on a street that happened to be one of the main roads leading to the football stadium where the town's official Fourth of July fireworks festivities would be held. I looked out the window and noticed a little American flag stabbed into my yard. Then I walked outside and saw that all the yards in front of all the houses on the street had little flags waving above the grass. The flags, according to a tag, were underwritten by a local real estate agency and the Veterans of Foreign Wars. I marched into the house, yanked out the phone book, found the real estate office in the yellow pages, and phoned them up immediately, demanding that they come and take their fucking flag off my lawn, screaming into the phone, "The whole point of that goddamn flag is that people don't stick flags in my yard without asking me!" I felt like Jimmy Stewart in *Mr. Smith Goes to Washington,* but with profanity. A few minutes later, an elderly gentleman in a VFW cap, who probably lost his best friend liberating France or something, pulled up in a big car, grabbed the flag, and rolled his eyes as I stared at him through the window. Then I felt dramatic and dumb. Still, sometimes I think the true American flag has always been that one with the snake hissing "Don't Tread on Me."

The week of the attack on the World Trade Center and the Pentagon, I watched TV news all day and slept with the radio on. I found myself flipping channels hoping to see the FBI handcuff a terrorist on camera. What did happen, a lot, was that citizens or politicians or journalists would mention that they wonder what it will be like for Americans now to live with the constant threat of random, sudden death. I know a little bit about what that's like. I did grow up during the Cold War. Maybe it says something about my level of cheer that I found this notion comforting, to remember that all those years I was sure the world might blow up at any second, I somehow managed to graduate from high school and do my laundry and see Smokey Robinson live.

Things were bad in New York. I stopped being able to tell whether my eyes were teary all the time from grief or from the dirty, smoky wind. Just when it seemed as if the dust had started to settle, then came the anthrax. I was on the phone with a friend who works in Rockefeller Center, and he had to hang up to be evacuated because a contaminated envelope had infected a person in the building; an hour later, another friend in another building was sitting at his desk eating his lunch and men in sealed plastic disease-control space suits walked through his office, taking samples. Once delivering the mail became life-threatening, pedestrians trudging past the main post office on Eighth Avenue bowed their heads a little

as they read the credo chiseled on the façade, "Neither snow, nor rain, nor heat, nor gloom of night stays these couriers from the swift completion of their appointed rounds."

During another war, across the river, in Newark, a writer turned soldier named Thomas Paine sat down by a campfire in September 1776 and wrote, "These are the times that try men's souls. The summer soldier and the sunshine patriot will, in this crisis, shrink from the service of their country; but he that stands it now, deserves the love and thanks of man and woman." In September and October, I liked to read that before I pulled the rubber band off the newspaper to find out what was being done to my country and what my country was doing back. I like the black and white of Paine's words. I know I'm no sunshine patriot. I wasn't shrinking, though, honestly; the most important service we mere mortal citizens were called upon to perform was to spend money, so I dutifully paid for Korean dinners and a new living room lamp. But still I longed for the morning that I could open up the paper and the only people in it who would irk me would be dead suicide bombers and retreating totalitarians on the other side of the world. Because that would be the morning I pulled that flag out of the recycling bin and taped it up in the window. And while I could shake my fists for sure at the terrorists on page one, buried domestic items could still make my stomach hurt—school prayer partisans taking advantage of the grief of children to circumvent the separation of church and state; the White House press secretary condemning a late-night talk show host for making a questionable remark about the U.S.

military: "The reminder is to all Americans, that they need to watch what they say, watch what they do, and that this is not a time for remarks like that." Those are the sorts of never-ending qualms that have turned me into the partly cloudy patriot I long not to be.

When Paine wrote his pamphlet, which came to be called "The American Crisis," winter was coming, Washington's armies were in retreat, the Revolution was floundering. His words inspired soldiers and civilians alike to buck up and endure the war so that someday "not a place upon earth might be so happy as America."

Thing is, it worked. The British got kicked out. The trees got cleared. Time passed, laws passed and, five student loans later, I made a nice little life for myself. I can feel it with every passing year, how I'm that much farther away from the sacrifices of the cast-off Indians and Okie farmers I descend from. As recently as fifty years ago my grandmother was picking cotton with bleeding fingers. I think about her all the time while I'm getting overpaid to sit at a computer, eat Chinese takeout, and think things up in my pajamas. The half century separating my fingers, which are moisturized with cucumber lotion and type eighty words per minute, and her bloody digits is an ordinary Land of Opportunity parable, and don't think I don't appreciate it. I'm keenly aware of all the ways my life is easier and lighter, how lucky I am to have the time and energy to contemplate the truly important things—Bill Murray in *Groundhog Day,* the baked Alaska at Sardi's, the Dean Martin Christmas record, my growing collection of souvenir snow globes. After all, what is happiness without cheap thrills? Reminds me of that passage in Philip Roth's novel *American Pastoral* when the middle-aged, prosperous grandson of immigrants marvels that his own daughter loathes the country enough to try to blow it up:

> Hate America? Why, he lived in America the way he lived inside his own skin. All the pleasures of his younger years were American pleasures, all that success and happiness had been American, and he need no longer keep his mouth shut about it just to defuse her ignorant hatred. The loneliness he would feel if he had to live in another country. Yes, everything that gave meaning to his accomplishments had been American. Everything he loved was here.

A few weeks after the United States started bombing Afghanistan and the Taliban were in retreat, I turned on the TV news and watched grinning Afghans in the streets of Kabul, allowed to play music for the first time in years. I pull a brain muscle when I try to fathom the rationale for outlawing all music all the time—not certain genres of music, not music with offensive lyrics played by the corrupters of youth, but any form of organized sound. Under Taliban rule, my whole life as an educated (well, at a state school), working woman with CD storage problems would have been null and void. I don't know what's more ridiculous, that people like that would deny a person like me the ability to earn a living using skills and knowledge I learned in school, or that they would deny me my unalienable right to chop garlic in time with the B-52's "Rock Lobster" as I cook dinner.

A few years back, a war correspondent friend of mine gave a speech about Bosnia to an international relations department at a famous midwestern university. I went with him. After he finished, a group of hangers-on, all men except for me, stuck around to debate the finer points of the former Yugoslavia. The conversation was very detailed, including references to specific mayors of specific Croatian villages. It was like record collector geek talk, only about Bosnia. They were the record collectors of Bosnia. So they went on denouncing the various idiotic nationalist causes of various splinter groups, blaming nationalism itself for the genocidal war. And of course a racist nationalism is to blame. But the more they ranted, the more uncomfortable I became. They, many of them immigrants themselves, considered patriotic allegiance to be a sin, a divisive, villainous drive leading to exclusion, hate, and murder. I, theretofore silent, spoke up. This is what I said. I said that I had recently flown over Memphis, Tennessee. I said that the idea of Memphis, Tennessee, not to mention looking down at it, made me go all soft. Because I looked down at Memphis, Tennessee, and thought of all my heroes who had walked its streets. I thought of Sun Records, of the producer Sam Phillips. Sam Phillips, who once described the sort of person he recorded as "a person who had dreamed, and dreamed, and dreamed." A person like Elvis Presley, his funny bass player Bill Black, his guitarist Scotty Moore (we have the same birthday he and I). Jerry Lee Lewis. Carl Perkins. Hello, I'm Johnny Cash. I told the Bosnian record collectors that when I thought of the records of these Memphis men, when I looked out the window at the Mississippi mud and felt their names moistening my tongue what I felt, what I was proud to feel, was patriotic. I noticed one man staring at me. He said he was born in some something-istan I hadn't heard of. Now that my globe is permanently turned to that part of the world, I realize he was talking about Tajikistan, the country bordering Afghanistan. The man from Tajikistan looked me in the eye and delivered the following warning.

"Those," he said, of my accolades for Elvis and friends, "are the seeds of war."

I laughed and told him not to step on my blue suede shoes, but I got the feeling he wasn't joking.

Before September 11, the national events that have made the deepest impressions on me are, in chronological order: the 1976 Bicentennial, the Iran hostage crisis, Iran-Contra, the Los Angeles riots, the impeachment trial of President Clinton, and the 2000 presidential election. From those events, I learned the following: that the Declaration of Independence is full of truth and beauty; that some people in other parts of the world hate us because we're Americans; what a shredder is; that the rage for justice is so fierce people will set fire to their own neighborhoods when they don't get it; that Republicans hate Bill Clinton; and that the ideal of one man, one vote doesn't always come true. (In the U.S. Commission on Civil Rights's report "Voting Irregularities in Florida During the 2000 Presidential Election," the testimony of Dr. Frederick Shotz of Broward County especially sticks out. A handicapped voter in a wheelchair, Dr. Shotz "had to use his upper body to lift himself up to get up the steps in order for him to access his polling place. Once he was inside the polling place, he was not given a wheelchair accessible polling booth. Once again, he had to use his arms to lift himself up to see the ballot and, while balancing on his arms, simultaneously attempt to cast his ballot.")

Looking over my list, I can't help but notice that only one of my formative experiences, the Bicentennial, came with balloons and cake. Being a little kid that year, visiting the Freedom Train with its dramatically lit facsimile of the Declaration, learning that I lived in the greatest, most fair and wise and lovely place on earth, made a big impression on me. I think it's one of the reasons I'm so fond of President Lincoln. Because he stared down the crap. More than anyone in the history of the country, he faced up to our most troubling contradiction—that a nation born in freedom would permit the enslavement of human beings—and never once stopped believing in the Declaration of Independence's ideals, never stopped trying to make them come true.

On a Sunday in November, I walked up to the New York Public Library to see the Emancipation Proclamation. On loan from the National Archives, the document was in town for three days. They put it in a glass case in a small, dark room. Being alone with old pieces of paper and one guard in an alcove at the library was nice and quiet. I stared at Abraham Lincoln's signature for a long time. I stood there, thinking what one is supposed to think: This is the paper he held in his hands and there is the ink that came from his pen, and when the ink dried the slaves were freed. Except look at the date, January 1, 1863. The words wouldn't come true for a couple of years, which, I'm guessing, is a long time when another person owns your body. But I love how Lincoln dated the document, noting that it was signed "in the year of our Lord one thousand eight hundred and sixty-three, and of the Independence of the United States of America the eighty-seventh." Four score and seven years before, is the wonderfully arrogant implication, something as miraculous as the virgin birth happened on this earth, and the calendar should reflect that.

The Emancipation Proclamation is a perfect American artifact to me—a good deed that made a lot of other Americans mad enough to kill. I think that's why the Civil War is my favorite American metaphor. I'm so much more comfortable when we're bickering with each other than when we have to link arms and fight a common enemy. But right after September 11, the TV was full of unity. Congressmen, political enemies from both houses of Congress, from both sides of the aisle, stood together on the Capitol steps and sang "God Bless America." At the memorial service at the National Cathedral, President and Mrs. Carter chatted like old friends with President and Mrs. Ford. Rudolph Giuliani, the mayor of New York, kissed his former opponent Senator Hillary Clinton on the cheek as the New York congressional delegation toured the World Trade Center disaster area.

In September, people across the country and all over the world—including, bless them, the Canadians, and they are born sick of us—were singing the American national anthem. And when I heard their voices I couldn't help but remember the last time I had sung that song. I was one of the hundreds of people standing in the mud on the Washington Mall on January 20 at the inauguration of George W. Bush. Everyone standing there in the cold rain had very strong feelings. It was either/or. Either you beamed through the ceremony with smiles of joy, or you wept through it all with tears of rage. I admit, I was one of the people there who needed a hankie when it was over. At the end of the ceremony, it was time to sing the national anthem. Some of the dissenters refused to join in. Such was their anger at the country at that moment they couldn't find it in their hearts to sing. But I was standing there next to my friend Jack, and Jack and I put our hands over our hearts and sang that song loud. Because we love our country too. Because we wouldn't have been standing there, wouldn't have driven down to Washington just to burst into tears if we didn't care so very, very much about how this country is run.

When the anthem ended—land of the free, home of the brave—Jack and I walked to the other end of the Mall to the Lincoln Memorial to read Lincoln's Second Inaugural Address, the speech Lincoln gave at the end of the Civil War about how "we must bind up the nation's wounds." It seems so quaint to me now, after September, after CNN started doing hourly live remotes from St. Vincent's, my neighborhood hospital, that I would conceive of a wound as being peeved about who got to be president.

My ideal picture of citizenship will always be an argument,

not a sing-along. I did not get it out of a civics textbook either. I got it from my parents. My mom and dad disagree with me about almost everything. I do not share their religion or their political affiliation. I get on their nerves sometimes. But, and this is the most important thing they taught me, so what? We love each other. My parents and I have been through so much and known each other for so long, share so many in-jokes and memories, our differences of opinion on everything from gun control to Robin Williams movies hardly matter at all. Plus, our disagreements make us appreciate the things we have in common all the more. When I call Republican Senator Orrin Hatch's office to say that I admire something he said about stem cell research, I am my parents' daughter. Because they have always enjoyed playing up the things we do have in common, like Dolly Parton or ibuprofen. Maybe sometimes, in quiet moments of reflection, my mom would prefer that I not burn eternally in the flames of hell when I die, but otherwise she wants me to follow my own heart.

I will say that, in September, atheism was a lonely creed. Not because atheists have no god to turn to, but because everyone else forgot about us. At a televised interfaith memorial service at Yankee Stadium on September 23, Muslim, Christian, Jewish, Sikh, and Hindu clerics spoke to their fellow worshipers. Placido Domingo sang "Ave Maria" for the mayor. I waited in vain for someone like me to stand up and say that the only thing those of us who don't believe in god have to believe in is other people and that New York City is the best place there ever was for a godless person to practice her moral code. I think it has something to do with the crowded sidewalks and subways. Walking to and from the hardware store requires the push and pull of selfishness and selflessness, taking turns between getting out of someone's way and them getting out of yours, waiting for a dog to move, helping a stroller up steps, protecting the eyes from runaway umbrellas. Walking in New York is a battle of the wills, a balance of aggression and kindness. I'm not saying it's always easy. The occasional "Watch where you're going, bitch" can, I admit, put a crimp in one's day. But I believe all that choreography has made me a better person. The other day, in the subway at 5:30, I was crammed into my sweaty, crabby fellow citizens, and I kept whispering under my breath "we the people, we the people" over and over again, reminding myself we're all in this together and they had as much right—exactly as much right—as I to be in the muggy underground on their way to wherever they were on their way to.

Once, headed uptown on the 9 train, I noticed a sign posted by the Metropolitan Transit Authority advising subway riders who might become ill in the train. The sign asked that the suddenly infirm inform another passenger or get out at the next stop and approach the stationmaster. Do not, repeat, do not pull the emergency brake, the sign said, as this will only delay aid. Which was all very logical, but for the following proclamation at the bottom of the sign, something along the lines of "If you are sick, you will not be left alone." This strikes me as not only kind, not only comforting, but the very epitome of civilization, good government, i.e, the crux of the societal impulse. Banding together, pooling our taxes, not just making trains, not just making trains that move underground, not just

171

making trains that move underground with surprising efficiency at a fair price—but posting on said trains a notification of such surprising compassion and thoughtfulness, I found myself scanning the faces of my fellow passengers, hoping for fainting, obvious fevers, at the very least a sneeze so that I might offer a tissue.

State of the Union

The Breakfast Club airs on cable every Saturday.

Every time you watch *60 Minutes* you learn about a horrible new way you can die.

This is how a three-year-old will tell a knock-knock joke:

> Knock, knock.
> Who's there?
> I've got a bug in my pocket!

In Chicago, McDonald's puts ketchup and mustard on the little hamburgers. But in New York City, there's no mustard, only ketchup.

You know who always has a good haircut? Meg Ryan.

On Halloween, you really can't go wrong with a gorilla suit.

There are two kinds of people in the world: the kind who alphabetize their record collections, and the kind who don't.

In his book *Christgau's Consumer Guide: Albums of the '90s*, the rock critic Robert Christgau, an alphabetizer if there ever was one, files the band Jon Spencer Blues Explosion under *S* even though there's an argument to be made for *J*.

In the criminal justice system, the people are represented by two separate yet equally important groups.

When Dolly Parton is in a room, everyone else looks sort of drab.

There are only two fruits native to North America and the cranberry is one of them.

In these fast and fickle times, it's nice to know that there are some things you can always count on: the enduring brilliance of the last page of *The Great Gatsby*; the near-religious harmonies of the Beach Boys' "California Girls"; and the lifelong friendship of Matt Damon and Ben Affleck.

If you just hear him on the radio, Senator Joseph Lieberman sounds exactly like the independent film director Jim Jarmusch, but without all the mentioning Johnny Depp.

Certain next-door neighbors were not big fans of the nine-CD Hank Williams boxed set.

Pittsburgh has a nice airport.

If you're an insomniac looking for an alternative to counting sheep and you come up with trying to remember your best memory in each state of the union, keep in mind that in order to remember your best memory you have to flip through a lot of bad ones, so that by the time you get to that time your friend's dad made you cry in Colorado, you're pretty much wide awake.

Jiffy Pop *is* as much fun to make as it is to eat.

Tom Landry, Existentialist, Dead at 75

The front-page obituaries honoring the former Dallas Cowboys head coach Tom Landry unimaginatively list only his most obvious achievements: Leading America's team to five Super Bowls between 1967 and 1988; playing and coaching for the New York Giants in the fifties; fathering three children; and staying married for fifty-one years. Oh, but his life had greater, more metaphysical manifestations. At least to me. Before Sartre, before Camus, there was Tom Landry. He introduced me to existentialism.

Tom Landry was my first entrée into dread: nagging, doubting, gnawing fear. And I'm not even referring to the '79 Super Bowl, in which I crumpled onto the living room carpet and wept as my beloved Cowboys—oh, Roger Staubach, quarterback, my quarterback—lost to the Pittsburgh Steelers. The wound is still so fresh that to this day I change the channel every time the then Steelers quarterback Terry Bradshaw's smug and shining pate pops out of my TV. (Can it be a coincidence that my own first love was the spitting image of Bradshaw and that he set my tender fifteen-year-old heart out to dry, only to hack it into strips of jerky, which he chewed up and swallowed in his pale green car while singing along with Frankie Goes to Hollywood?) Oh, I learned things from the '79 Super Bowl—disappointment, upset, dashed dreams, et cetera—but those things combined do not necessarily add up to existentialism proper. (I also learned, just weeks before the game, at Christmas, that my mother had no understanding of the NFL, what with its separate players and teams and all, because when she sent a football for Roger Staubach to sign for me it came back with his signature—beautiful penmanship— but also covered in Dallas Cowboys stickers due to the fact that the ball my mother had sent Staubach to sign was a Joe Namath, so Namath's name was blocked with little gray and blue helmets. And despite this faux pas, Staubach sent me framed team pictures two years in a row. Would Terry Bradshaw have been that gracious, that forgiving? Would he?) No, the existentialism came up in the off-season, as I read my Tom Landry Christian comic book.

My Pentecostal youth was awash in salvation testimonials that consistently backfired. Meant to inspire young Protestants with tales of redemption, more often than not these books and films and stories clued me in to the horrors of the world. I learned of knife fights from the Pat Boone flick *The Cross and the Switchblade*; of paralysis from the story of Joni, a girl who had her spine snapped in a diving accident, got saved, and then had a promising art career by painting flowers and things with a brush stuck between her teeth; of the Holocaust when I was five as my mother read Corrie ten Boom's *The Hiding Place*, in which Dutch Christians hid Jews; and from my Landry comic book I had my first inkling of the being and nothingness that was my birthright. In the comic, Landry, in signature coat and hat, looked back on his youth. He said that as a player he won games. He said that he fell in love, got married, had children, became a coach. And then, he said the thing that shocked me. He said that despite the wins, the love, the success, the family, he said that *something was missing*. That is, until he accepted Jesus Christ as his personal savior. But before that, *something was missing*. I gasped. I thanked the Lord for my certainty, which was the certainty of Tom Landry—faith in God, in the Cowboys, in America. It never occurred to me that something might be missing, and so I prayed every night that when I grew up, nothing would be missing. Prayed that prayer every night up until the day I lost my faith in God. And, Tom Landry would be happy to know, something has been missing ever since, different things at different times. If not love, then success, if not success, then supplies. Who hasn't known the terror of that moment when you're baking the cake and the oven is preheated and you've mixed in everything, creamed the butter with the sugar, floured the pans, only to realize that you're out of baking powder? Every day, I wake up and wonder, What will be missing today? Looking back on Landry's work in the theory of something-is-missingness, I am reminded of the words of his existential colleague Jean-Paul Sartre, who wrote, "Man is condemned to be free."

And to die. Rest in peace, Tom Landry. Something is missing and it's you.

The Strenuous Life

As a little girl, I was jealous of Teddy Roosevelt. I did not envy his presidency or his valor on the battlefield. What I wanted was his asthma. Theodore Roosevelt is one of my father's heroes. So when my sister and I were children, Dad would tell us stories about TR's buffalo hunts and the Rough Riders' charge up San Juan Hill. He would tell us how this brave, tough hunter and soldier was born a wheezing New York City four-eyes.

"All little Teddy Roosevelt could do," my dad would say of the asthmatic rich boy, "was stay in bed and read."

"Ew," said my sister.

Sigh, said I. Getting to stay in bed and read all day was what I was shooting for. The only childhood ailment I landed was a hearing problem, and when you have tubes in your ears, your parents still force you to go outside and play in the dirt with your sister.

Dad would continue, little Teddy Roosevelt toughened himself up by doing exercises. He came out West to become a rancher and really learned how to breathe. Later on, I would come to admire little Teddy Roosevelt's daintier accomplishments, such as civil service reform. But every parable has a lesson, and I suspected that my dad was aiming these wuss-turned-hero tales in my direction. Despite all evidence to the contrary, like my need as a three-year-old to wash my hands sixty-five times a day, he just kept on believing I would toughen up, right up until the night in 1984 I came home from the movies raving about a Woody Allen film called *Broadway Danny Rose*.

Years later, I moved to New York City, to an apartment on Twenty-first Street. My first week here I walked by a house on Twentieth. The plaque next to the door said it was the birthplace of Theodore Roosevelt. I laughed out loud. (The National Park Service operates the house, which makes the tour extra fun in that you're being shown around fancy parlors straight out of Edith Wharton by a park ranger dressed to ride into the Grand Canyon on a mule.) The stifling house Teddy Roosevelt longed to escape, I'd spent my whole life running toward. Except that now, the shut-in's life in New York City is even better than I imagined as a child, because these days, there's the Internet. Now, you don't even have to walk outside to go to the library.

One morning, I began my day, as is my habit, perusing the wire service reports on America Online. I do this for two reasons. First, I like to get the straight news before *The New York Times* contaminates my brain. And, second, I adore the AOL headlines. "Bush Reminds Parents to Love Kids," said one. A story about the heavyweight champ–convicted rapist was titled "Tyson: Women Don't Like Me." Though my personal favorite remains "Still No New Gun Control Laws." Scrolling through the wires on June 26, 2001, an Associated Press headline caught my eye, "N. Dakota May Seek Name Change":

> BISMARCK, N.D. (AP) North Dakotans can't move their state to warmer climes, but some hope a proposed name change will at least help the state seem a little less northern. The Greater North Dakota Association, the state's chamber of commerce, is backing a proposal to cut the state's name to "Dakota." Supporters insist the plan would help alter the state's image as a frigid, treeless prairie.

Pathetic, I thought. If North Dakota is that desperate for tourist dollars, then I'm going to give them some. I called my sister in Montana immediately, asking if she and my nephew would like to come with me to North Dakota for the weekend.

"I guess," she answered. "If you want."

Montanans do not, as a rule, vacation in North Dakota. In fact, there is a cottage industry of jokes about the diminished intellectual capacity of the North Dakota neighbors. Such as, two North Dakotans are building a rocket to the sun. When they are informed that they and their rocket will burn up before they even land on the sun's surface they reply, "We'll be okay. We'll just go there at night." A Montanan is capable of making up North Dakota jokes on the spot. My parents, for example, were having a garage sale at their Bozeman home. My father hoped to sell a wheelbarrow he bought at someone else's garage sale the previous summer. He bought it for ten bucks, he tells a potential buyer, so he's selling it for five, because, he quips, "I attended the North Dakota School of Business."

"I'm from North Dakota, too!" the woman exclaimed, asking him what town the business school is in.

According to that AP article about the state changing its name, "Lee Peterson, the governor's economic development director, didn't believe the name was a major factor in people's assumptions about North Dakota. 'The problem with North Dakota is that no one knows about us,' Peterson said." That is true. I grew up next door to North Dakota, and the only thing I know about it is that Lawrence Welk comes from there. So imagine my surprise when I went to North Dakota's official state tourism Web site and the first image on the screen is the face of Theodore Roosevelt next to the quote, "I never would have been President if it had not been for my experiences in North Dakota."

Huh. Teddy Roosevelt lived in North Dakota? The western land where he became a man in my father's stories was North Dakota? I always thought it was Wyoming—some breathtaking landscape where present-day movie stars buy ranches. I pictured TR riding a horse around the sort of craggy Rocky Mountain terrain where Harrison Ford could swoop in and rescue hikers in his helicopter.

I met my sister and nephew in Billings, and we drove to

Medora, North Dakota, and Theodore Roosevelt National Park. The first thing we see in the park is Roosevelt's log cabin. It's been moved from its original site on the Maltese Cross Ranch and plopped down in the visitor center backyard. It's beautiful—raw but cozy, with a rocking chair by the door and a buffalo hide bedspread that is so spectacular I find myself wishing they sold them in the Pottery Barn catalog.

Roosevelt fled to the Dakota Territory in 1884, when, within twenty-four hours, Valentine's Day coincidentally, his mother died and Alice, his wife, died in childbirth. He mourned Alice for years. He must have lain sleepless and grieving in this bedroom. Devastated, Roosevelt moved here to the Badlands. The place looks like a broken heart. The harsh and solitary buttes and ravines have been beaten up by eons of wind. Everything's bleak in color but for the burnt red of coal veins struck by long-ago lightning. "When one is in the Bad Lands," Roosevelt wrote, "he feels as if they somehow *look* just exactly as Poe's tales and poems *sound*." As my sister drives past a windy rock pile, I can picture Roosevelt slumping home to his rocking chair at night, reading Poe's poem about *his* dead wife, "That the wind came out of the cloud by night / Chilling and killing my Annabel Lee."

"Nowhere, not even at sea, does a man feel more lonely than when riding over the far-reaching, seemingly never-ending plains," Roosevelt wrote of the Dakota landscape. "And, after a man has lived a little while on or near them, their very vastness and loneliness and their melancholy monotony have a strong fascination for him. Nowhere else does one seem so far

off from all mankind; the plains stretch out in death-like and
measure-less expanse, and as he journeys over them they will
for many miles be lacking in all signs of life."

Deathlike, melancholy monotony: Roosevelt's writings on
the place, while quotable, must be a mixed blessing for North
Dakota's press agents. Every superlative he uttered is modified
by reality. "Grim beauty," for example, gets a lot of play. In the
North Dakota Department of Tourism brochure, the sort of
sunset photo I'd imagine departments of tourism live for is
marked with a Roosevelt epitaph about how "nothing could be
more lonely"—there's that word again—"and nothing more
beautiful than the view at nightfall across the prairies to these
huge hill masses."

Amy drives us around the South Unit of the park, past
prairie dog towns and weird vistas and wild horses. After a
while, we pull off the road. Amy puts Owen in a backpack, and
we go for a hike. The trail winds through rocks and brambles.
Echinacea grows wild beside the path. We're the only ones
here, and at a thick patch of brush I make Amy take my picture, not because it's particularly beautiful, though it is, or because I'm having a good time, though I am. I just want a
record of me standing here, so far from where I live.

We get back in the car, and we're on the road maybe two
minutes when we get out again to gape at a bison. We had already seen a whole herd of them, but there is something more
noteworthy about one lone, dark animal standing still, perfectly framed in front of a little beige butte. It is so still, in fact,
that I understand how easy it must have been for those white
hunters in the nineteenth century to pop off buffalo for fun

from the windows of passing trains. How could anyone kill anything so magnificent, I wonder as we head into the town of Medora for lunch. A lunch, I confess, of tasty buffalo burgers.

My sister and I get to talking about hunting. I've never been, but Amy used to be quite the marksman. There are photos of her all over our dad's shop, a smiling eighth-grader standing over her bleeding quarry. A gunsmith, Dad made her a .22 for Christmas when we were ten, the year he built me a dollhouse. I ask her what it was like to go hunting with Dad. At first, she says, she loved it. She liked hiking and poking around in the mountains with him. She liked it up until the day she shot an antelope and it didn't die right away. She panicked, watching it writhe around in pain. She fetched Dad, who had to shoot it twice in the head just to finish it off. By the next time they went hunting, for deer, she still hadn't gotten over that antelope. She kept her lingering guilt to herself. Dad sat her on the top of a hill and went down below to scare deer in her direction. This maneuver worked. A deer walked right up to her, but she shooed it away before Dad could find out, whispering, "Get out of here! Go away!" She didn't want to kill again.

"Jesus," I say. She was out there in the freezing mountains learning about life and death and the dire food chain when I was back home screwing around with my dollhouse and its tiny windup piano that played Beethoven.

The passenger seat of a car my sister is driving as we dissect our shared childhood is the most comfortable place in the world. She's in charge, does everything, and my only job is to bring the music—I'm going through a Ricky Nelson phase—

and keep her awake. I am the flighty twin. She's the one who drives cars and gives birth and bakes pies. She rolls her eyes when I tell this story, because it ends with me saying, "And I was the special surprise baby," but our parents didn't know they were having twins. In the womb, Amy and I had the same heartbeat. Mom gave birth to Amy, and the doctor said, "There's another one in there." It's silly, but I think knowing that has been the driving force of my whole life. I always thought of myself as the extra kid. Not in a bad way, I just thought Amy could do everything a daughter is supposed to do—go hunting and produce a grandchild—and anything I could contribute to my parents' parental hopes would be gravy, a bonus.

Lately, the contrast between my life and my sister's has widened. A few months ago she moved from Bozeman, the relatively urbane college town where we grew up, to a remote county in the middle of Montana that boasts of hosting "more deer and elk than people." Amy's husband, a soil scientist, got transferred there. Employed by the U.S. Department of Agriculture, my brother-in-law is the only person I know who's still making money off the New Deal.

When I went to visit my sister's family, the first thing I saw upon entering her "town" was a bunch of tumbleweeds blowing down Main Street. It's a two-hour drive from any sort of civilization. The closest attraction is an abandoned mining camp about which a historical marker states, "The Silver Panic of 1893 caused the town to die a rapid death."

Amy's house, which looks out at a ring of mountains and sits next to a Forest Service road perfect for hiking, is just the

189

sort of isolated mountain home that city folks dream about when the car alarms go off. On the other hand, I called her one morning and asked what she was up to and she answered, "Making bagels." It took me a second to figure out that she was actually *making bagels,* because she can't buy them there so she's boiling the dough from scratch just like the pioneers used to do.

One of the interesting effects of my sister's move to nowhere is that we've never been closer. Partly that's because I'm worried about her stuck out there so I call her all the time, but it's also because, curiously, we now have so much in common. Our common bond is that we both live in extreme places where, if you're at all given to reflection, you constantly question where and how you live. In Manhattan, I lack spaciousness and nature and quiet; in the sticks, she lacks choices and culture and bagels.

Every now and then my sister will say something that reminds me how she's so much more western than I am. On the phone recently, she was recounting some local skirmish involving a "lawman," and I interrupted her midsentence, asking, "Did you just say 'lawman,' Amy? Are you talking about a cop?"

I have the same sorts of dislocating moments talking to our father. Boning up for my trip west, I read Roosevelt's book *Hunting Trips of a Ranchman.* Describing it to Dad, I mention that I'm nervous about going to Theodore Roosevelt National Park. In three separate passages, Roosevelt remarks how plentiful the rattlesnakes are around there, and that one of them killed a little girl when it bit her in the ankle and then she fell down from the pain and it bit her again in the neck. I've always had a thing about snakes.

"That reminds me of this one time I went snake hunting," Dad replies. "I caught this rattler and I was holding his jaw shut. He got so mad that he wrapped himself tight around my arm. I was wearing cowboy boots, though, and I slipped and hit my head on a rock and knocked myself out. I woke up and I was just lying there on the ground looking up at the sky. Then I remembered, 'Seems like I had me a snake.' I looked down at my arm and the snake was still wrapped around it, only he'd gotten so mad that he tried to bite me, but he bit himself instead. He bit himself so hard that one of his fangs came out and got lodged in his own body. The fang was just stuck there poking out of his flesh. Now he's *really* mad and he's writhing and he's only got one fang left in his mouth and he's coiled himself even tighter around my arm. So the only way I can get him to let go of me is to take out my pistol and just shoot him off my arm."

When you are a westerner living on the East Coast, this is just the sort of folksy anecdote the city slickers expect you to tell. But I was the worst Montanan in history. My one blood and guts yarn, a mountain biking accident in which I woke up in an ambulance, involves hitting a parked car at an intersection because I was spacing out about an art history project on the way home from the library. In fact, as an adult, I've become so enamored with our national parks because I want the federal government to intervene between nature and me—to protect me from myself, to build sidewalks and guardrails and post big signs that say SNAKE CROSSING or KEEP OUT.

The only halfway rustic stories I have about my former life on the eastern slope of the Continental Divide all take place at one of my many dumb minimum-wage jobs. The closest thing I have to a cowboy story is being a motel maid during the College National Finals Rodeo and swabbing up out-of-town calf ropers' Coors beer vomit. Come to think of it, my interaction with the Rocky Mountain landscape was limited to my participation in the service industry economy built around others' enjoyment of said landscape. I made your supper when you got back from rock climbing. I cleaned your motel room while you toured Yellowstone. I baby-sat your kids while you went hiking in the Spanish Peaks. And, at the ski hill bar, I listened to you rave about how "the powder was *awesome!*" as I handed you your beer—unless you were Canadian, in which case it was a grudgingly mixed White Russian or a glass of Clamato, an appalling mixture of tomato juice and clam.

In 1905, Theodore Roosevelt delivered a speech in Chicago called "The Strenuous Life." It begins, "I wish to preach, not the doctrine of the ignoble eases, but the doctrine of the strenuous life, the life of toil and effort, of labor and strife." It is remarkably similar to the speech my parents delivered to my sister and me the summer before eighth grade. The gist of it was "You're thirteen, now get a job." So we worked part-time at a day-care center looking after kids not much younger than we were. I think I resented it at the time, and I've never been able to enjoy apple juice since, but knowing at such an early age what hard work can mean was an annoyingly valuable lesson.

Souvenir shopping in Medora, I observe the girl working

the cash register at a gift shop and think, That's the person I used to be, watching the clock while tourists take time off. I give her my credit card and buy my nephew an official Teddy Roosevelt teddy bear outfitted in the uniform the Rough Riders wore to fight the Spanish in Cuba. I hand it to him, chirping, "Here's your imperialism stuffed animal, Owen!" He promptly sets out to rip the wire-rim glasses off the bear's face. Our little Rough Rider is fifteen months old and living so strenuously that I have been leaving 40 percent tips at restaurants all over town to cushion the blow of the post-Owen, post-apocalyptic cleanup.

Medora's claim to fame is the "Medora Musical," an outdoor, amphitheater musical revue "dedicated to the memory of America's twenty-sixth president." Perky regional song and dance folk reenact the charge up San Juan Hill. The narrator of the musical says that Theodore Roosevelt "was a man who was close to the American heart. His spirit is right here, right now, all around us in Medora. You can see what he saw. You can be inspired by what inspired him. And even on the wind you can hear his voice. It is challenging every single one of you." This is hokey and yet, I find, true. My whole life, no matter how happy I am I've always had this nagging feeling that Teddy Roosevelt is looking over my shoulder whispering, "Is this all you are?" As is my policy toward all well-rounded people, I sort of hate him a little. Roosevelt was a well-read heman, a bookworm and an athlete, a robust outdoorsman who loved to come home from the hunt and crack open a volume of Hawthorne. He was a jock and a nerd at the same time. As Elting Morison puts it in his introduction to Roosevelt's autobiography, "He is certainly the only President who read *Anna Karenina* while on a three-day search for cattle thieves."

I like my life in the East, but maybe the most western thing about me is that I feel guilty about liking it. What if I'm perfectly content that, on any given day, my only communion with the earth is watching the sun set over New Jersey or burning a "geranium jasmine oak moss" aromatherapy candle?

I find myself talking about this on the phone one day with my friend Matt, a fiction writer who lives in Washington, D.C. Maybe writers obsess over the urban versus rural dilemma more than most because we can live anywhere. "Living in the country as opposed to living in the city," he mentions. "That's a big theme in my life. My father had grown up in Harlem. We lived in the country and we spent a lot of time smelling the air. You weren't supposed to be inside if the sun was shining. He preached to me that 'The land is what we're here for, son.'"

How does this jibe, I ask, with the way Matt spends his days—writing short stories about bad boyfriends in a rented office in the basement of the Uraguayan Embassy?

Matt says, "D.C. just sucks all the way around, so anyone who lives here is always thinking about moving somewhere else. My wife would like to move to London or Los Angeles or New York City. She loves cities. But I keep coming up with reasons why we should go live near trees. We'll be walking along and I'll say something like, 'You know how your mind just unwinds when there are no cars around?'"

He asks me if I ever go camping. "Oh, God, no," I answer. "I've never been camping." (That's not true. I went camping once with my college boyfriend. It was uncomfortable and boring. We ended up driving to the nearest town to watch the Republican National Convention on the television at a pizza place. Because who wants to stare at a bunch of stars when you can witness Dan Quayle accepting the nomination for vice president?)

Matt continues, "An astrologer once told me, 'You suffer from what's called a geographic.' A geographic is when a person walks around thinking that where he lives will make his life better. The astrologer said, 'Let me tell you, life is about an emotional connection to people and things and it doesn't matter where you are on the globe.'"

"So," I ask, "was that it for you? You just decided to make yourself at home then and there?"

"Mostly, but some days I just want to move to Mexico and learn how to make clothes out of the dirt around my house."

"I know what you mean," I say. "Only I don't want to move to Mexico and play in the dirt. It's more like I want to want that. I like how things are, so I worry that I'm not aiming high enough. I worry that I'm too complacent. I worry that I'm missing out on all the Mexican dirt in the world because I'm perfectly happy sitting in my leather chair watching HBO."

"Ah, but when you bought your leather chair," he tells me, "that's when I knew you were on a roll."

I mention that one night, not long after I got home from North Dakota, I was sitting in that very leather chair, watching television. An old movie came on, *The Best Man*. The film is adapted from a Gore Vidal play about the two front-runners in a presidential primary. The striking opening credits superimpose the names of cast and crew over images of every U.S. president from Washington on down. Theodore Roosevelt is the first one who laughs. I shook my head and grinned at the picture of the crinkle-eyed, openmouthed President Teddy. That guy really knew how to live.

ACKNOWLEDGMENTS

Geoffrey Kloske at Simon & Schuster willed this book into being and cajoled it to completion, taking every last one of my many, many phone calls even though he is equipped with caller ID. Other editors and producers who pitched in include my beloved Ira Glass, Julie Snyder, and Alex Blumberg at *This American Life*; Dave Eggers at *McSweeney's*; Paul Tough at *Open Letters*; Andy Ward at *Esquire*; Barrett Golding at *Hearing Voices*; Andrew O'Hehir and Bill Wyman at *Salon*; Rodes Fishburne and Owen Edwards at *Forbes ASAP*; and Daniel Ferguson and Conan O'Brien at *Late Night with Conan O'Brien*. Along with the interviewees, these people helped: Todd Bachmann, Kevin Baker, Steven Barclay, John Flansburgh, Nicole Francis, Robin Goldwasser, Nicole Graev, Jack Hitt, Nick Hornby, Matt Klam, Joel Lovell, Greil and Jenny Marcus, Katie Martin, Doug Petrie, Kate Porterfield, David Levinthal, David Rosenthal, David Sedaris, Stephen Sherrill, and my agent, Wendy Weil. Special thanks to Bennett Miller for taking me to Gettysburg, Matt Roberts for taking me to Salem, and Ben Karlin for taking me to the movies. David Rakoff deserves an exclamation point! My love and apologies to my family—Pat, Janie, Amy, Jay, and Owen.

SARAH VOWELL is the author of *Take the Cannoli* and *Radio On* and a contributing editor to public radio's *This American Life*. She lives in New York City.